THE DECLINING ECONOMIC STATUS OF BLACK CHILDREN

Cynthia Rexroat

D1475834

Joint Center for Political and Economic Studies
Washington, D.C.
1994

The Joint Center for Political and Economic Studies contributes to the national interest by helping black Americans participate fully and effectively in the political and economic life of our society. A nonpartisan, nonprofit institution founded in 1970, the Joint Center uses research and information dissemination to accomplish three objectives: to improve the socioeconomic status of black Americans; to increase their influence in the political and public policy arenas; and to facilitate the building of coalitions across racial lines.

Opinions expressed in this volume are those of the authors and do not necessarily reflect the views of the other staff, officers, or governors of the Joint Center or of the organizations supporting the Center and its research.

Copyright © 1994 by the Joint Center for Political and Economic Studies.

Joint Center for Political and Economic Studies
1090 Vermont Avenue, N.W., Suite 1100
Washington, D.C. 20005–4961

All rights reserved.
Printed in the United States of America.
British Cataloging in Publication Information Available.

Library of Congress Cataloging-in-Publication Data

Rexroat, Cynthia.

The declining economic status of Black children : examining the change / by Cynthia Rexroat.
p. cm.
Includes bibliographical references.
1. Afro-American children—Economic conditions. 2. Poor children—United States. 3. Afro-American families. I. Title.
E185.86.R48 1993
330.973'0089'96073—dc20 93–44354 CIP

ISBN 0–941410–95–1 (cloth : alk. paper)
ISBN 0–941410–96–X (pbk. : alk. paper)

Foreword

Few issues before the nation are more pressing than the plight of children in poverty. Nearly half of all black children in the United States today live below the poverty line, and many of their families are becoming poorer. The most impoverished black children are the very youngest—babies and toddlers. Unless current trends are reversed, most children in the highest-risk families can expect to spend their childhood in poverty.

The urgency of this problem, together with the lack of sufficiently detailed information regarding its character and scope, prompted the Joint Center for Political and Economic Studies to undertake an in-depth study. Our efforts were made possible by the generous support of the Carnegie Corporation of New York, the Ford Foundation, and other funders. The research for this study was conducted by Dr. Cynthia Rexroat, a former Joint Center research associate who is currently associate professor at the Center for Research on Women, Memphis State University.

To provide our understanding of childhood poverty with greater clarity and depth, Dr. Rexroat examined changes over a long period, 1960 to 1985. This made possible an analysis of the impact that changing economic conditions have had on earnings and employment for young household heads. The resulting findings have implications for the current review taking place in state and federal legislatures of community development initiatives and employment and training programs. Whether the focus is empowerment zones for the redevelopment of our urban communities or welfare reform to promote independence, consideration needs to be given to the likely impact of new policies on black children and youth.

Moreover, the policy implications go far beyond the black community. While African Americans have borne the brunt of declining economic opportunity, young white families with children have also been faced with diminished economic prospects. Finding solutions to the problems of those most in need can provide guidance for improving the lives of all Americans.

It is our hope that this research will clarify some of the aspects of black poverty that have been misunderstood, will stimulate greater public concern about children in poverty, and will elicit renewed resolve on the part of policymakers for a sustained effort to improve the lives of America's most valuable resource—its children.

Dr. Rexroat's work was carried out under the supervision of the Joint Center's vice president for research, Dr. Milton Morris, and our director of research programs, Dr. Margaret Simms. Yukiko Carnes was the computer programmer/analyst on the project. Editing and production were completed under the direction of John Clemons, vice president for communications, and Nancy Stella, former director of communications. We are particularly grateful to Marc DeFrancis, Jane Lewin, Allison King, Merlinda Novicio, and Tyra Wright, who contributed to the editing, proofreading, and design of this book.

> Eddie N. Williams
> President
> Joint Center for Political
> and Economic Studies

CONTENTS

LIST OF TABLES

1
Introduction

In the 1960s, the African American community looked forward to an era of economic opportunity and upward mobility that would flow out of the Civil Rights movement. But in the 1990s, evidence indicates that a growing segment of the black population is increasingly mired in poverty. Despite legal guarantees of equal opportunity and genuine occupational mobility for members of the expanding black middle class, the aggregate figures on black family income and poverty have changed very little. If anything, they seem to be getting worse—especially for black families with children. If current trends hold, black children in poor families will be increasingly hard-pressed to overcome the burdens imposed by poverty. Growing numbers of them will not succeed.

The increasing poverty among African American children is commonly associated with changes in family structure that have taken place since 1960—more specifically, with the dramatic increase in the number of female-headed families and in the proportion of out-of-wedlock births. Because black child poverty has been rising at the same time that family structure has been changing, the latter is widely assumed to be the cause of the former.

The research reported here was undertaken to examine the validity of that assumption. Our study findings in some instances confirm and in others confound conventional wisdom about black poverty. As expected, female-headed families and out-of-wedlock births are strongly linked to growing childhood poverty. However, changes in family structure do not alone account for the growing impoverishment of black children. In fact, family structure is probably not even the most significant factor in the growth of black child poverty.[1] Nor do changes in family structure explain why black children are more likely to be persistently poor than white children, or why black children who live in intact two-parent families throughout their childhood are as likely to be poor as white children who spend their entire childhoods in single-parent families.[2]

The study demonstrates that declining economic opportunity probably plays a greater part in the growing prevalence of childhood poverty among African Americans than does changing family structure. By examining economic and other factors that are simultaneously affecting family income levels, this analysis sharpens our understanding of the deteriorating economic status of these children and of the role that changing family structure actually plays in that decline.

Focus of This Study

The study examines changes in the economic well-being of African American children and their families over the period from 1960 to 1985, looking at overall trends and at a range of factors that may be affecting these same trends.

The questions that the study addresses concern, first, some things that we "know" to be true but for which we have lacked empirical support, and second, the extent to which experiences differ for different groups within the black population. Chief among the questions addressed are these:

(1) How do economic conditions differ for children in different regions of the country? How have these differences changed?

(2) To what extent is the increased poverty among black children associated with changes in family structure?

(3) Are children in certain age groups more likely to be poor than others? And how likely are poor black children to "grow out of" their poverty as they get older?

(4) Do all children in female-headed families face similar conditions, or is their economic well-being affected by such factors as their mothers' age and previous marital status?

(5) To what extent is growing child poverty the result of economic factors unrelated to family structure, such as the availability of employment, prevailing wage levels, or public assistance levels?

Importance of the Study

The economic well-being of African American children requires urgent attention because impoverishment in childhood carries lifetime consequences, such as low educational and career attainments. [3] If left unaddressed, racial disparities in economic status—with all the inequities, loss of productivity, and social costs that are implied—are likely to remain a permanent feature of American society.

It is this concern that drives policymakers and leaders in the black community to seek effective solutions for the problem of black child poverty. Nevertheless, no set of policies, however well-intentioned, can do the job unless the problem is correctly diagnosed in the first place. There is common agreement that changes in family structure have contributed to the increase in poverty among black children. But very little is known about the extent to which family structure accounts for this increase and, therefore, very little is known about which policies could change either family structure or poverty among particular types of families. In addition, we need more information on regional differences and on the changing dimensions of child poverty over time, in order to target programs in a cost-effective manner. This study contributes new and significant detail to our understanding, identifies some areas for future research, and points to some strategies that must be more fully developed if we are to make headway in improving the well-being of black children and the families in which they live.

Organization of the Study

This monograph looks at individual economic and demographic trends in terms of their effects on poverty among African American children. It also describes how these trends have combined to make them more economically vulnerable in recent years.

Chapter two first looks at overall trends in the economic well-being of black children between 1959 and 1984 and then compares regional as well as urban-rural trends. Chapter three provides a broad overview of the relative influence of changing family structure and changing economic conditions on trends in the poverty rate of black children. Chapter four examines in more detail changes in black family structure, some of the reasons for the changes, and ways in which the changes have altered the living arrangements and economic status of black children.

Because a child's economic well-being is determined by that of his or her family, the next two chapters look at the changing

3

economic status of black families over the same time period, and some of the reasons for such changes. Chapter five analyzes the ways in which the economic status of each family type has changed, including the growing divergence between families headed by single (that is, never-married) women and families headed by divorced women. Chapter six examines the extent to which changes in four factors that affect family income have altered levels of economic well-being among black families of different types (the four factors are number of earners in families, geographic location, family income from public assistance, and age of family head). Chapter seven concludes the volume and outlines several policy strategies for addressing the growing problem of persistent child poverty.

Sources of Data

The data used here come from the decennial U.S. censuses for 1960, 1970, and 1980 and from mid-decade information from the Current Population Survey. While these data do not allow us to follow individual families and children over time, they do give us sufficient information to answer some questions and examine issues that could not be addressed by the smaller longitudinal data sets available.

Unless otherwise indicated, all tables and figures come from the one-percent micro data samples of the 1960, 1970, and 1980 (Sample B) censuses and the March annual demographic file of the 1985 Current Population Survey. These data can provide detailed information that is unavailable in published sources. For instance, the P-60 series of the Current Population Reports, which shows annual income and poverty data for children in female-headed families, does not differentiate between mothers who have never married and mothers who are divorced. This omission is misleading, since nearly two-fifths of all black children in female-headed families have unmarried mothers, and their economic status is much more precarious than that of children whose mothers are divorced.[4]

In addition to providing a national overview, the study examines changes in the economic status of black children by region and for 45 metropolitan areas that had a black population of at least 100,000 in 1980. These cities, 11 of them in the Midwest, six in the Northeast, three in the West, and 25 in the South, were home to over half of the nation's black population in 1980. (See the boxed list on page 5.)

4

By combining a comprehensive national portrait with this more detailed information by region and metropolitan area, the study provides for the first time a detailed "map" of poverty. Whereas data at the national level frequently mask regional and urban-rural variations, the more detailed findings obtained through this approach demonstrate that black child poverty differs substantially by region. Throughout the monograph, comparisons are made to white children whenever possible. Because of the high cost of processing data for these years, it was not always feasible to analyze white families in the same way as black families. However, the published data that were available concerning whites are included here.

Metropolitan Areas Examined in This Study

Northeast
Boston
Buffalo
New York
Newark
Philadelphia
Pittsburgh

South
Atlanta
Augusta
Baltimore
Baton Rouge
Birmingham
Charleston, S.C.
Charlotte
Columbia, S.C.
Dallas/Fort Worth
Fort Lauderdale
Greensboro
Houston
Jackson
Jacksonville
Louisville
Memphis
Miami

Mobile
Nashville
New Orleans
Norfolk
Richmond
Shreveport
Tampa/St. Petersburg
Washington, D.C.

West
Los Angeles
San Diego
San Francisco

Midwest
Chicago
Cincinnati
Cleveland
Columbus
Dayton
Detroit
Gary
Indianapolis
Kansas City
Milwaukee
St. Louis

Definition of Terms

For general readers not already familiar with the demographic terminology and measurements used throughout this book, a brief review may be helpful. Due to the nature of this book, unless otherwise indicated all generalizations about children and their families refer to blacks.

Family Type

Divorced mother, a term used throughout this study, is a shorthand term that refers to any mother who was formerly married, and therefore includes widowed mothers as well (though widows make up only a very small proportion of this population).

Single mother, by contrast, identifies only a mother who has never been married.

Single parent, in this monograph, refers to a mother heading a family alone; while fathers are occasionally single parents as well, their occurrence is still so infrequent that excluding them does not affect the statistical portrait of children.

Married-couple family and **two-parent family** are terms that are here used interchangeably.

Children in families refers to all individuals under the age of 18 who are related to the household head by birth, marriage, remarriage, or adoption. This is the same category that the U.S. Census Bureau uses when it speaks of a household head's "own children."

Related children is a broader category that includes nephews, nieces, grandchildren, and any other related children living in a household.

Income

Poverty. Two definitions of poverty are used in this study, the federal government's definition as well as a modified definition (since the study concerns children "at risk"). Where not otherwise stated, the definition being used is the federal one. The threshold line for the modified definition is 125 percent of the official poverty line. Families whose income is above but within 25 percentage points of the official poverty threshold are considered by most analysts to be "near poor" and to be most in danger of slipping below the official poverty line.

Working poor denotes families in poverty that derive more than 50 percent of their income from earnings.

Dependent poor denotes families in poverty that derive 50 percent or more of their income from public assistance.

Geography

Rural vs. urban; metro vs. nonmetro. In Census terminology, **rural** is used interchangeably with **nonmetro** and **urban** with **metro**. This book follows that usage. Therefore, a suburban area that lies within the boundaries of a Census SMSA (standard metropolitan statistical area) is counted as an urban, metro locale (and not as a rural or nonmetro locale).

2

The Changing Economic Status of Black Children

T his section presents a national overview of how African American children fared economically between 1959 and 1984 by focusing on their poverty rates and the extent to which their family incomes are derived from earnings and public assistance. It then examines changes in the economic status of these children by region, metropolitan area, and residence in urban or rural area, because national-level data generally mask the diverse experiences of population subgroups. In combining a comprehensive national portrait with this more precise information, the study provides a detailed "map" of black child poverty.

National Trends in Black Child Poverty, 1959-1984

The data show that in the 25 years after 1959, poverty rates for black children fluctuated but were consistently above 35 percent. More than four out of every ten black children—46.8 percent—were poor in 1984.

Economic conditions steadily improved for black (and white) children between 1959 and 1979 but took a sharp downturn between 1980 and 1984. During this same 25-year period, the percentage of black children who depended on welfare also sharply increased. The steepest increases in poverty were felt by black children under age three.

By way of definition, the government officially classifies families and individuals as poor by using a "poverty index" designed by the Social Security Administration in 1964 (and revised by the Federal Interagency Committees in 1969 and 1980).[1] The poverty line is updated each year to reflect changes in the cost of living. In 1984, the average poverty threshold was $8,277 for a family of three and $10,609 for a family of four.[2]

Improving Economic Conditions for Black Children, 1959-1979. During the 20 years from 1959 to 1979, child poverty among African Americans declined 27 percentage points, on average, from 64.8 percent to 37.9 percent. The percentage of white children in poverty also declined. Improved economic well-being for children of both races coincided with increased national prosperity, governmental promotion of goals such as equal employment opportunity,[3] and the expanded social programs that were part of the Johnson administration's "War on Poverty."

Growing Impoverishment Among Black Children, 1979-1984. The trend lines changed direction between 1979 and 1984, when poverty overtook increasing percentages of black (and white) children. This period also saw major changes in economic conditions, including the severe 1981-1982 recession, the decline in real family income for young families (beginning in the mid-1970s), and the falling real value of public assistance.

The Deteriorating Economic Status of Black Children Under Age Three. Aggregate-level trends mask variations among children of different ages. In fact, the very youngest African American children—the under-three's—became especially vulnerable economically between 1979 and 1984 (see Table 2.1). Before 1979, black children of all ages were equally likely to be poor but by 1984, over half of all black children under three were poor an increase of over 10 percentage points in only five years. Thus, the under-three's in 1984 were both the poorest black children and those with the fastest-rising poverty rates. This is a significant departure from previous eras.

Growing Welfare Dependency Among Black Children, 1969-1984. For a growing number of poor black children and their families, during the 1970s and 1980s public assistance was increasingly likely to replace earnings as the primary source of family income. As a result, the percentage of black children in "dependent poor" families rose during this period, while the percentage of those in "working poor" families fell.

Dependent-poor families are defined here as those who receive half or more of their total income from public assistance and who are below 125 percent of the poverty level. Working-poor families are those in which more than one-half of total family income comes from earnings and who are below 125 percent of the poverty level.

Because the working poor tend to be in jobs that are most affected by general economic downturns, during periods of economic stagnation or decline working-poor families are much more likely than non-poor families to turn to public assistance. Thus, as Table 2.2 shows, the proportion of all black children who lived in non-poor families declined in 1984 to its 1969 level (about 46 percent), after having increased as a result of the severe recessions the United States experienced during the mid-1970s and the early 1980s, but the proportion of all black children who lived in dependent-poor families nearly doubled during this same period (going from 11.3 percent to 21.4 percent). In other words, the balance between children in working-poor and children in dependent-poor families had changed markedly. In 1969, about 3.5 times as many black children lived in working-poor families as in families dependent on public assistance (around 40 percent and 11 percent, respectively). By 1984, this ratio had shrunk to 1.5 (33 percent and 21 percent, respectively).

Regional Trends in Black Child Poverty, 1969-1984

Overview. Across the United States, areas experience different rates of growth and decline and, thus, regional and local economic conditions are a significant factor in the economic well-being of black children. During the 1970s, the well-being of African American children steadily improved in Southern cities even while it was eroding substantially in cities elsewhere. A black child living outside the South was more likely to be poor in 1984 than in 1969, and more likely to rely on welfare. A Southern black child, in contrast, was likely to be slightly better off in 1984 than in 1969; and Southern black children below the poverty line were more likely in 1984 than in 1969 to be in working-poor rather than dependent-poor families. These changes correspond to the shifts in the regions' economies during that period.

Until 1970, the Midwest and Northeast far outpaced the South in economic growth and prosperity. From 1970 to 1980, however, the older industrial regions began to lose manufacturing and other blue-

9

collar jobs,[4] but service jobs—custodians, cashiers, and clerks, for example—were not being created fast enough to replace the lost manufacturing jobs.[5] Thus, for the general population, unemployment rates rose sharply in the Midwest and Northeast while employment rates declined. In most urban areas outside the South, black child poverty was rising.[6]

In the South, however, large gains in general employment were being made in the trades and administrative services, and modest gains occurred in manufacturing.[7] Compared with the urban Northeast and Midwest, therefore, many Southern metropolitan areas experienced larger increases in black female employment, smaller declines in black male employment, greater growth in real family income—and consequently lower poverty rates for black children. About three-quarters of all black families with children in the United States live in urban areas.

Percentages of Urban Black Children in Poverty, Southern and Non-Southern, 1969-1979. In 1980, nearly 60 percent of all black children lived in 45 standard metropolitan statistical areas (SMSAs) with black populations of at least 100,000. About 40 percent of such children were in the South.[8] In 1969, large Southern cities had much higher percentages of black children in poverty than did urban areas in the Northeast and Midwest.

In 1969, 30 percent of black children in the 20 SMSAs outside the South were poor, compared with 43 percent in the 25 SMSAs inside the South.[9] By 1979, however, following a decade in which black child poverty declined by 14 percent in Southern cities and rose by 17 percent in Northern cities, the average poverty rate of black children was 35 percent for the SMSAs outside the South and 37 percent for Southern SMSAs.[10]

Types of Poverty Among Urban Black Children, 1969-1979. Data at the national level for the period from 1969 to 1979 show that black children were coming to be better off, primarily because many families were rising from working-poor to non-poor (as seen in the aggregate data in Table 2.2). As Figure 2.1 shows, however, this trend was at work only in Southern cities, where more black children rose above 125 percent of the poverty line.

The opposite was occurring in cities outside the South, where black children—whether above or below 125 percent of the poverty

Figure 2.1
Change in Poverty Status of Black Children Between 1969 and 1979:
Southern vs. Non-Southern Metropolitan Areas*

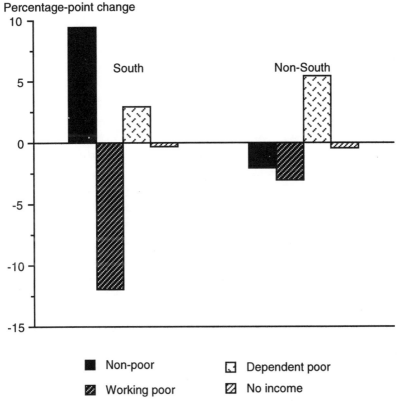

Percentage-point change

■ Non-poor   ▣ Dependent poor

▨ Working poor   ▨ No income

* Based on the analysis of 45 standard metropolitan statistical areas.

line—were becoming poorer. In non-Southern metropolitan areas, the percentage of dependent-poor black children was increasing, as many families were moving downward from both working-poor and non-poor status. Thus, the regional gap in urban poverty was shrinking. By 1979, the average proportion of non-poor black children was 54 percent for Southern urban areas and 58 percent for urban areas outside the South.

In the 20 urban areas outside the South, the proportion of black children above the poverty line declined 2 percentage points; the proportion in working-poor families declined 3 percentage points;

11

and the proportion that depended on public assistance grew by more than 5 points. Outside the South, poverty rates declined only in Kansas City (Mo.), Los Angeles, Pittsburgh, and St. Louis.

Midwestern metropolitan areas were the hardest hit, reporting a 7.2 percentage point increase in dependent-poor black children between 1969 and 1979, compared with a 3.4 percentage point increase in Northeastern SMSAs. In some cities (in both regions), black children suffered especially sharp setbacks. In Milwaukee and Cincinnati, for example, the percentage of black children in dependent-poor families increased by approximately 11 points, and in Buffalo the increase was 10 points.

Even in the few Northeastern and Midwestern metropolitan areas where the percentage of black children above 125 percent of the poverty line was holding steady, the relative status of black children already classified as poor nevertheless changed substantially. In these metropolitan areas, the declining proportion of children in working-poor families and the increasing proportion in dependent-poor families usually balanced each other out. In Indianapolis, for instance, the proportion of working-poor children fell by 10.1 percentage points, while the proportion of dependent-poor children rose by 10.9 points.

In contrast, in the South the poverty rate for black urban children declined, as mentioned earlier, from 43 percent to 37 percent, rising only in Atlanta, Birmingham, and Jacksonville. Expansion in the region's economy seems to have enabled many black family heads to improve their earnings. The 9.5 percentage point increase in the proportion of black children who were above 125 percent of the poverty line coincided with the region's 12 point decline in children whose families had been working-poor.

Comparing Regional Trends in Child Poverty, 1979 and 1984. It was not possible to analyze metropolitan areas beyond 1979. [11] For the period 1979 to 1984, therefore, the trends discussed here are limited to regional and urban-rural comparisons.[12] Because of the nationwide recession of 1981-1982, during the early 1980s the numbers of poor black children rose throughout the country. But whereas in the South this increase took the form of growth in the category of the working poor, in the North it meant more children among the dependent poor.

Figure 2.2
Percentage of Black Children in Poverty, Urban Midwest vs. Rural South: 1969, 1979, 1984

Percentage

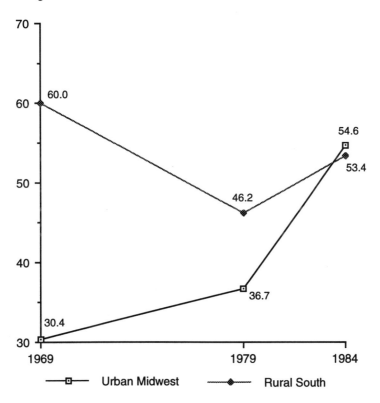

Both the prevalence and the degree of poverty among black children increased most sharply in the Midwest (see Figure 2.2 and Tables 2.3 and 2.4). There, black child poverty increased nearly 50 percent. By 1984, therefore, black children in the South and Northeast were equally likely to be poor but much less likely to be poor than their Midwestern counterparts.

In the South, most of the increased child poverty seemed to involve shifts from non-poor to working-poor status (see Table 2.4).

13

However, children in the Northeast and Midwest apparently plunged more deeply into poverty, going from non-poor to dependent poor. In the Midwest, 37 percent of all black children relied on public assistance in 1984, up from 20 percent in 1979. The respective percentages rose for the Northeast from 21 to 31 percent; for the South, from 10.5 to 12.5 percent. Whereas in 1979 poor black children in these Northern areas were as likely to be working poor as dependent poor, by 1984 they were considerably more likely to be dependent poor.

The Economic Status of Urban versus Rural Children, 1979-1984. In 1984, just as in 1979, black children in the South were considerably more likely to be poor if they lived in rural areas rather than in urban areas. These findings are consistent with previous research showing that during the 1970s and 1980s, rural Southern blacks did not benefit as much as their urban counterparts from the substantial growth in nonagricultural employment.[13] Nevertheless, black children in the rural South fared somewhat better economically than black children in some urban areas outside the South. Between 1979 and 1984, for instance, the poverty rate for these children in Northeastern cities increased by nearly 24 percent, but grew by only 15.6 percent in Southern rural areas[14] (Table 2.5). As Figure 2.2 shows, the poverty trend for black children in the urban Midwest is particularly striking in relation to that for their counterparts in the rural South. In 1969, those living in the rural South were twice as likely to be poor as those in the urban Midwest. Ten years later, in 1979, the difference had shrunk to about 25 percent. By 1984, the proportion of poor children in the rural South was virtually the same as that in the urban Midwest (53.4 percent and 54.6 percent, respectively).

The vast majority of rural black families live in the South; about two-fifths of all Southern black children live in rural areas. Since Southern rural blacks have long been one of the most economically disadvantaged population groups in the United States,[15] these figures expose the full magnitude of the economic downturn experienced by Northeastern and Midwestern blacks. As Lichter (1989) reports, black employment hardship[16] in the North nearly doubled between 1970 and 1985 (going from 20.1 percent to 39.5 percent), while comparable hardship levels in the rural South increased only

14

5 percent (going from 44.3 percent in 1970 to 46.5 percent in 1985).

Outside the South, the rate of increase in black child poverty was largely the same in urban areas as for each region as a whole (see Tables 2.3 and 2.5). This is not surprising, since nearly all black children in these regions live in urban areas. Within the South, poverty among black children increased at the same rate (15.8 percent) in both rural and urban areas.

Table 2.6 shows the percentage of poor black children by type of poverty in their respective urban and rural locations for 1979 and 1984. The urban and regional patterns were very similar outside the South (Tables 2.4 and 2.6). Within the South, however, the percentages of urban and rural children who were dependent poor fell into a pattern different from that in other regions.

On the regional level, increased poverty among black children in the South (from 1979 to 1984) resulted largely from growth in the category of working poor. However, this was the case primarily for children in the rural South. As Table 2.6 shows, between 1979 and 1984 the proportion of black children in the rural South classified as working poor rose by 5 percentage points, while the proportion shown as dependent poor increased by only 1.6 points. But the small increase in poverty among poor black urban children stemmed from nearly equal increases in the working-poor and dependent-poor categories (2 and 1.8 percentage points, respectively).

15

Table 2.1

Percentage of Black Children in Poverty by Age Group: Selected Years, 1959 to 1984

Age of Children	1959	1969	1979	1984
0 to 2 years	64.8%	41.6%	41.0%	52.7%
3 to 5 years	65.8	42.5	40.3	49.5
6 to 17 years	64.5	42.5	36.7	44.5

Table 2.2

Distribution of Black Children by Poverty/Dependency Status[a]: 1969, 1979, 1984

	1969	1979	1984
Not in poverty	46.6%	53.5%	45.3%
Working poor[b]	39.8	29.8	32.8
Dependent poor[c]	11.3	14.8	21.4
No Income	2.3	1.9	0.5
Total	100.0%	100.0%	100.0%
Total (in 1,000s)	(9,227)	(9,234)	(9,151)

[a] Poverty defined here as having income below 125% of the official poverty threshold.
[b] More than half of total family income is derived from earned income.
[c] Half or more of total family income is derived from public assistance.

Table 2.3

Poverty Rates and Population Distribution of Black Children, by Region, 1979 and 1984

	Northeast	Midwest	South	West	Total Children (in 1,000s)
1979 [a]					
Poverty rate	37.1%	36.7%	39.4%	30.2%	8,940
Pop. distribution[b]	(18.4%)	(20.4%)	(53.3%)	(7.9%)	
1984					
Poverty rate	45.7	54.2	45.2	40.4	9,151
Pop. distribution	(18.1)	(20.6)	(53.5)	(7.8)	

[a] Figures for 1979 exclude the 2,976 children whose region of residence was not identified in the one-percent Public Use Sample.
[b] Measured as the percentage of all black children in the U.S. who live in each specific region.

Table 2.4

Poverty/Dependency Status* of Black Children, by Region, 1979 and 1984

	Non-Poor		Working Poor		Dependent Poor	
	1979	1984	1979	1984	1979	1984
Northeast	55.0%	46.5%	21.8%	22.4%	21.0%	30.7%
Midwest	56.7	38.6	21.3	24.1	20.2	37.1
South	50.8	46.2	36.9	40.8	10.5	12.5
West	62.5	54.3	20.6	24.9	14.7	19.0

* Poverty defined here as having income below 125% of the official poverty threshold.

Table 2.5

Percentage of Black Children in Poverty, by Region* and Metro/Nonmetro Area, 1979 and 1984

	Northeast Metro	Mid-west Metro	South Metro	South Nonmetro	West Metro	*Total (in 1,000s)*
1979	37.1%	36.7%	35.5%	46.2%	30.3%	8,825
1984	46.0	54.6	39.4	53.4	40.8	8,823

* The region of residence was not identified for 4.4% of black children in 1980 and 3.6% in 1985.

Table 2.6

Poverty/Dependency Status* of Black Children, by Region and Metro/Nonmetro Area, 1979 and 1984

	Non-Poor		Working Poor		Dependent Poor	
	1979	1984	1979	1984	1979	1984
Northeast metro	54.9%	46.2%	21.8%	22.9%	21.1%	30.4%
Midwest metro	56.8	38.6	21.1	23.0	20.2	38.2
South metro	55.3	52.4	32.1	34.1	10.4	12.6
South nonmetro	42.5	37.2	45.2	50.3	10.8	12.4
West metro	62.4	54.8	20.5	22.5	14.9	20.6

* Poverty status defined here as having income below 125% of the official poverty threshold.

3
Family Structure vs. Economic Conditions: Their Relative Impact

T he degree of economic hardship faced by African American children in the United States has clearly varied across regions and across urban and rural settings. However, regardless of where they live, a growing number of them are likely to be poor. This section examines the extent to which the overall poverty rate of black children is affected by changing family structure and by changing economic conditions.

The Impact of Changing Family Structure

The increase in black child poverty is commonly associated with changes in family structure that have taken place since 1960—more specifically, the dramatic increase in the number of female-headed families. Because black child poverty has been rising at the same time that family structure has been changing, it is widely assumed that the latter is the cause of the former. As Figure 3.1 shows, between 1960 and 1985 the proportion of black children who lived in married-couple families substantially declined relative to the proportion who lived in female-headed families.

In 1960 most black children lived in two-parent families; that is, nearly 3.5 times as many children lived in families headed by married couples as lived in families headed by women. Twenty years later, in 1980, the proportion of all black children living in female-headed families was almost as great as the proportion living in two-parent families. And by 1985, considerably fewer black children lived in married-couple families than in female-headed families. Because female-headed families tend to be more economically vulnerable

Figure 3.1
Relative Distribution (Ratio*) of Black Children Between Married-Couple and Female-Headed Families: 1960, 1970, 1980, 1985

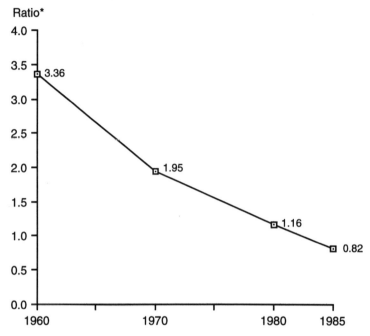

*Ratio of the proportion of black children in married-couple families to the proportion in female-headed families.

than married-couple families, it seems plausible that the sharp rise in the number of black families headed by women has contributed to increased poverty among black children.

The Impact of Changing Economic Conditions

It seems likely, however, that increasing child poverty among African Americans may also be linked to changes in factors other than family structure—factors such as varying employment prospects for workers in different age groups, or varying economic conditions across regions of the country. For instance, black families and their children living in regions that had experienced economic decline would have faced fewer employment opportunities, lower real wage

Figure 3.2
Relative Poverty Rate of Black Children, Female-Headed Compared to Married-Couple Families: 1959, 1969, 1979, 1984

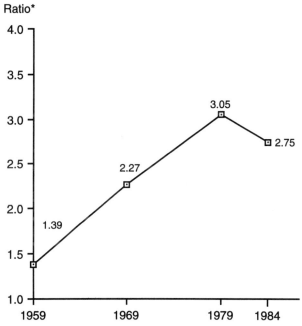

*Ratio of povery rate of black children in female-headed families to poverty rate of black children in married-couple families.

levels, and consequently higher poverty rates than families living in more prosperous regions.

More importantly, if female-headed families had been more likely than two-parent families to have faced limited economic opportunity, we would expect this to widen the gap in black child poverty by family type, which in turn would increase the overall rate of child poverty, given the growth in families headed by women.

As Figure 3.2 shows, the economic status of black children in different family types did change dramatically between 1959 and 1984. In 1959, the poverty rate of black children in female-headed families was 1.4 times as great as that of children living with both parents. From the late 1970s to the mid-1980s, however, black

21

children living in female-headed families were about three times as likely to be poor as those living in married-couple families. Clearly, the economic circumstances faced by different family types have diverged over time and may have contributed to the growing impoverishment of black children.

Weighing the Relative Effects of Changing Family Structure and Changing Economic Conditions on Black Child Poverty

The worsening economic status of black children appears to be the result of changing family structure and changes in the economic conditions faced by different family types that have occurred between 1959 and 1984. Figure 3.3 shows how much lower the poverty rate of black children would have been if changes in family structure had not occurred (scenario 1) or if the economic status of various types of families had changed equally (scenario 2).

Scenario 1 shows that if family structure had not changed after 1960 (that is, if the percentage of black female-headed families had not risen at all) but poverty rates for each family type had continued to change as they actually did over the time period, then in 1979, 29 percent of all black children would have been poor instead of the actual 38 percent; in 1984, 34 percent would have been poor instead of the actual 47 percent. Scenario 2, however, shows that if female-headed families had been able to "hold their own" (that is, if their poverty rates had changed in the same way that the poverty rates changed for married-couple families after 1959), only 24 percent of all black children (rather than the actual 38 percent) would have been poor in 1979, and 30 percent (instead of 47 percent) would have been poor in 1984—even with the increased proportion of children living in female-headed families.

These data indicate that although changes in family structure contributed to the higher rates of poverty among black children, changes in the economic conditions faced by different family types probably played an even greater role in the worsening economic status of these children. The following chapters detail these changes and show how they have resulted in the growing impoverishment of black children.

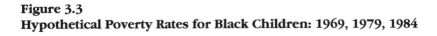

Figure 3.3
Hypothetical Poverty Rates for Black Children: 1969, 1979, 1984

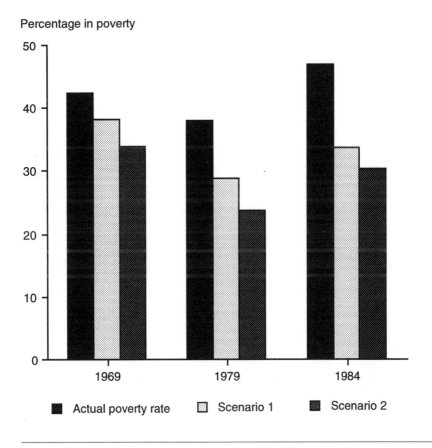

4
The Impact of Family Structure on Child Poverty

AccOrding to today's conventional wisdom, the "deterioration" of the black family is largely responsible for the failure of the black community to make greater economic advances and, more important, is likely to perpetuate a cycle of poverty for future generations of blacks. It is predicted that children who experience the consequences of marital instability—children who are born to unmarried women and raised in a one-parent household—will be apt to repeat these behaviors when they reach adulthood, thus further widening the gap between black and white family structure and economic status.

Published statistics for the past 30 years would seem to bear out these distressing predictions. Recently, many more black children (61 percent) than white children (15 percent) have been born out of wedlock.[1] On average, black children born in recent years will also spend more of their childhood (12 years) in one-parent families than will white children (7 years).[2] Moreover, nearly three of every six black children, compared with fewer than one of every six white children, are living in poverty.[3] By the mid-1980s, black children, who were just 15 percent of the total child population, constituted 32 percent of the population of poor children.[4]

It is not surprising, then, that policymakers and scholars continue to link growth in the number of female-headed families and in rates of out-of-wedlock childbearing with the widening economic gap between black and white children. Indeed, a much higher proportion of black children (54.6 percent) than white children (15.9 percent) live in female-headed families,[5] and the median income of

25

such black families is only one-third that of black married-couple families.[6]

The number of black families with children in the United States increased dramatically in the 25 years from 1960 to 1985, going from 2.5 million in 1960 to nearly 4.5 million. The percentage of black families with children has also increased, going from 60 percent in 1970 to about 67 percent in 1985.[7]

However, the total number of black children increased more modestly (from nearly eight million in 1960 to over nine million in 1970). Since 1970, their number has stood at around nine million. The average number of children per family has declined steadily across all family types, with female-headed families showing about a 25 percent decline and married-couple families a 33 percent decline. In 1985, the average number of related children per family was 2.05 for married-couple families, 2.14 for families headed by divorced, separated, or widowed women, and 1.94 for families headed by single (never-married) women.

The Growth in Number of Black Female-Headed Families

While all types of families with children have grown in number, growth in the number of female-headed families (and in the number of children who live in these families) has been especially dramatic. The proportion of black families headed by women doubled between 1960 and 1985 (from 25 percent in 1960 to over 50 percent). This doubling was due to the rising proportion of births to single women as well as increasing rates of separation and divorce and declines in women's rates of remarriage.

During the final 15 years of that period, most of the growth in "female headship" stemmed from the increasing proportion of all black families headed by "single" women, who had never married (as opposed to those who were separated, widowed, or divorced). In 1970, about 17 percent of all mother-only families were headed by single women; in 1985 the figure was 38 percent.

These changes in patterns of marriage and childbearing have drastically shrunk the proportion of children who live in two-parent families: from almost three-fourths of all black children in 1960 to fewer than one-half (43.4 percent) by 1985. The other side of this coin is that by 1985, 52.7 percent of all black children were living in female-headed families. This included the 19 percent of the total who were in families headed by single women—up from just over 2 percent in 1960.

Demographic Factors Behind the Rising Percentage of Births to Single Women. Various demographic changes (see Table 4.1) have contributed to the increase in the number of black families headed by single women, particularly women in their 20s.[8]

First, as the baby boomers entered their 20s and 30s, there were simply more black women than ever before in their prime childbearing years. Second, more of them have postponed marriage or forgone it altogether, thereby lengthening the time during which they are at risk for an out-of-wedlock birth. As a result, in both 1980 and 1985, nearly 60 percent of all single mothers were in their 20s, whereas before 1980 a large majority of them were age 30 or older.[9]

Third, birth rates have been falling much faster among married than among unmarried black women,[10] even though the declining "nonmarital birth rate" (the number of births per 1,000 unmarried women) shows that unmarried black women in their 20s were having significantly fewer babies in 1985 than in 1970 (they were also having babies at much lower rates than their married counterparts). At the same time, the "out-of-wedlock birth ratio" for women in their 20s (the percentage of all live births to single women) more than doubled between 1970 and 1985. This dramatic jump in the percentage of births to single women is due largely to the rapid growth in the number of black women in their 20s, combined with the sharp increase in the percentage who remained single.

Changes in the Living Arrangements of Black Children

These changes in family structure have transformed the living arrangements of black children. In 1985, black children of all ages were far more likely than in 1960 to live in female-headed families and to reside in independent households instead of extended families. Preschoolers, in particular, had become far more likely to live with single mothers.

The Increasing Concentration of Young Children in Single-Parent Families. In 1985, 25 percent of all black under-threes lived in families headed by single women (up from fewer than 3.0 percent in 1960), with another 26.8 percent living in families headed by women who were divorced. Table 4.2 shows comparable changes for children ages 3 to 5 (about 33 percent of all black children in 1985, compared with about 40 percent in 1960). In 1985, among children ages 6 to 17, 16.3 percent lived with single mothers and 37.1 percent with divorced mothers, up from 2.0 percent and 23 percent, respectively, in 1960.

The Trend Toward Independent Rather Than Extended-Family Households. Since 1960, about 70 percent of black married-couple families have included related adults, but female-headed families (and particularly those headed by single mothers) are increasingly less likely to include adult relatives. In 1960, about 44 percent of families headed by both single and divorced women included other adults. By 1985, however, the comparable figure was 41 percent for divorced mothers and only 15 percent for single mothers.

This trend is consistent with data showing the changing distribution of children who are related to the heads of their households. The proportion of all related children who are "own children" (defined by the Census Bureau to include not only direct offspring but step-children and adopted children under 18 years) varied by family type from 1960 to 1985. Table 4.3 shows that about 90 percent of all children in two-parent families were "own children" in most years. In contrast, the proportion of "own children" in families headed by single women increased from 77.4 percent in 1960 to 92.3 percent in 1985, while the proportion in families headed by formerly married women fell from 82 percent in 1970 to 72.2 percent in 1985.[11]

The Deteriorating Economic Status of Black Children With Single Mothers

The increasing concentration of black children in independent households headed by single mothers has contributed to the overall growth in black child poverty. Whereas the percentage of black children in poverty declined from 1959 to 1979, Figure 4.1 shows that black children who lived in two-parent families (where poverty rates fell 39 percentage points) were far more likely to escape poverty during this period, than were black children in families headed by divorced women (who showed a 27 percentage-point drop) or in families headed by single women (a 17 percentage-point drop).

Figure 4.1 also documents the striking divergence in economic

Figure 4.1
Percentage of Black Children in Poverty by Family Type: 1959, 1969,
1979, 1984

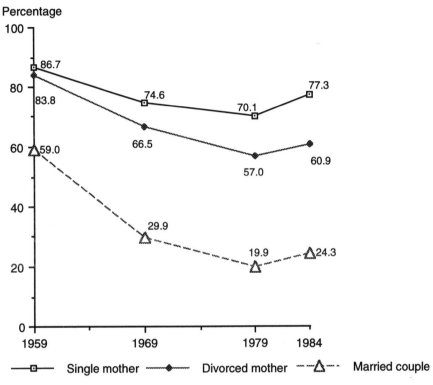

Percentage

Legend: Single mother — Divorced mother — Married couple

well-being between children of single mothers and children of divorced mothers. In 1959, children in both family types were about equally likely to be poor. But by 1979, 70 percent of black children in families headed by single women were poor, compared with 57 percent of children in families headed by divorced women.

Although the poverty rate increased for black children across all family types between 1979 and 1984, the increase was largest for children of single mothers, followed by children of married parents and finally by children of divorced women. As a result of these trends, the children of single mothers were far more likely to be impoverished (77.3 percent) in 1984 than were children of divorced

29

mothers (60.9 percent) or married parents (24.3 percent). The possible effects of different factors (e.g., the lower ages of single mothers, and the declining real earnings for workers in their 20s) on the growing economic gap between these family types are discussed in chapter six.

Growing Welfare Dependency Among Black Children With Single Mothers. Children of single mothers were the most likely to depend on public assistance, as Table 4.4 shows. Only a small fraction (about 2.5 percent) of all black children in two-parent families depended on public assistance throughout the period analyzed. By contrast, about 25 percent of children with divorced mothers and about 40 percent of children with single mothers were dependent poor in both 1969 and 1979.[12] By 1984, the percentages of dependent-poor children in mother-only families had increased still more: to about 30 percent in families headed by formerly married women and to over 50 percent in families headed by never-married women.

Growing Vulnerability of Black Children Under Age Three With Single Mothers

Between 1979 and 1984, children under three in all family types came to be increasingly worse off than older children. As Table 4.5 shows, however, young children with single mothers experienced sharper declines in their economic circumstances than young children in other family types. By 1984, children under three with single mothers had the highest poverty rate of all: 87 percent compared with 65 percent for those with divorced mothers and 26 percent for those in two-parent families.

Increasing Welfare Dependency of Children Under Age Three. The evidence thus far suggests that the economic vulnerability of children born to single mothers is increasing, and this is particularly true for the youngest children. Table 4.6 shows the striking increase in the proportion of young children of single mothers who are dependent on public assistance, as the percentage of dependent poor rose from 43.5 percent in 1969 to 63.2 percent in 1984.

In 1969, these young children were only slightly more likely to be dependent poor than older children, regardless of their family type. In 1979, this was still true for under-30s in married-couple families, but very young children in female-headed families were more likely than older children to be dependent poor, especially if their mothers had never married. Thus among black children who lived with a single mother in 1984, 63.2 percent under the age of three were dependent poor, compared with 53.7 percent of children of all ages.

This age-group difference is not due to any significant increase in under-threes as a proportion of all children living in these households; children under three represented 22.1 percent of all children with single mothers in 1970, compared with 22.5 percent in 1985. Rather, these youngest children are increasingly likely to live in families headed by women, especially women who have never married—and these are the families that are increasingly likely to be poor.

Black children in female-headed families are not only more likely to be poor than those with married-couple parents, they are also more likely to be poor than they used to be (especially those with single mothers). The deteriorating economic status of these families compared with that of other family types has occurred because single mothers are increasingly more likely than divorced or married women to be in their 20s (a disproportionately disadvantaged age bracket), unemployed, or employed at low-wage jobs, and are even less likely than divorced women to receive child support payments from absent fathers.[13] As a result, income levels of families headed by single women have not kept pace with income levels of other family types.

Table 4.1

Marital Status and Birth Rates for Black Women Ages 20-24 and 25-29, 1970 and 1985

	Women Ages 20-24		Women Ages 25-29	
	1970	1985	1970	1985
Births to nonmarried women (per 1,000 women)	131.5	116.1	100.9	81.4
Births to married women (per 1,000 women)	263.2	228.3	148.3	136.7
Out-of-wedlock birth ratio*	31.3%	64.3%	20.3%	44.2%
Total number of women (in 1,000s)	973	1,453	769	1,420
Percentage of age group that has never married	43.3%	76.2%	19.0%	51.9%

* The percentage of all live births that were to unmarried black women in specified age group.
Sources: U.S. Bureau of the Census, 1970; 1985c. National Center for Health Statistics 1972; 1987a; 1987b.

Table 4.2

Age Distribution of Black Children by Family Type: 1960-1985, Selected Years

Age of Children and Family Type (by head)	1960	1970	1980	1985
Children 0 to 2 years				
Married couple	77.4%	65.9%	53.1%	44.4%
Formerly married woman	17.8	22.1	24.0	26.8
Never-married woman	2.7	7.9	18.1	25.0
*Total**	97.9%	95.9%	95.2%	96.2%
Total (in 1,000s)	(16,148)	(13,548)	(14,649)	(15,561)
Children 3 to 5 years				
Married couple	75.8%	64.8%	52.3%	43.4%
Formerly married woman	19.6	24.5	26.1	28.1
Never-married woman	2.5	7.3	17.7	23.1
*Total**	97.9%	96.6%	96.1%	94.6%
Total (in 1,000s)	(15,653)	(14,882)	(13,647)	(15,450)
Children 5 to 17 years				
Married couple	72.1%	62.0%	51.4%	43.2%
Formerly married woman	23.0	29.7	34.8	37.1
Never-married woman	1.8	4.2	10.1	16.3
*Total**	96.9%	95.3%	96.3%	96.6%
Total (in 1,000s)	(46,583)	(63,916)	(64,082)	(60,497)

* Columns do not total 100% because children in male-headed families are not included.

33

Table 4.3

Distribution of Black Children in Families by Relationship to Household Head and Family Type: 1960, 1970, 1980, 1985

Family Type (by head)	1960	1970	1980	1985
Married couple				
Own children	86.8%	90.0%	89.3%	89.1%
Other related children	13.2	10.0	10.7	10.9
Total	100.0%	100.0%	100.0%	100.0%
Total (in 1,000s)	(5,794)	(5,816)	(4,779)	(3,975)
Formerly married woman				
Own children	71.8%	82.0%	79.4%	72.2%
Other related children	28.1	18.0	20.6	27.8
Total	99.9%	100.0%	100.0%	100.0%
Total (in 1,000s)	(1,667)	(2,565)	(2,937)	(3,094)
Never-married woman				
Own children	77.4%	87.2%	89.1%	92. 3%
Other related children	22.6	12.8	10.8	7.7
Total	100.0%	100.0%	100.0%	100.0%
Total (in 1,000s)	(165)	(486)	(1,154)	(1,730)
Male				
Own children	59.5%	71.0%	71.7%	62.0%
Other related children	40.5	29.0	28.3	38.0
Total	100.0%	100.0%	100.0%	100.0%
Total (in 1,000s)	(211)	(361)	(364)	(351)

Table 4.4

Distribution of Black Children by Family Type and Poverty[a]/ Dependency[b] Status: 1969, 1979, 1984

Family Type (by head) and Poverty Status	1969	1979	1984
Married couple			
Not in poverty	59.0%	72.9%	69.4%
Working poor	38.2	23.9	28.0
Dependent poor	2.2	2.5	2.4
No income	0.5	0.7	0.2
Total	99.9%	100.0%	100.0%
Total (in 1,000s)	(5,816)	(4,779)	(3,975)
Formerly married woman			
Not in poverty	23.6%	33.2%	29.9%
Working poor	44.3	38.6	39.7
Dependent poor	26.9	25.2	29.5
No income	5.2	3.0	0.9
Total	100.0%	100.0%	100.0%
Total (in 1,000s)	(2,565)	(2,937)	(3,094)
Never-married woman			
Not in poverty	17.5%	22.9%	17.8%
Working poor	34.2	31.1	27.9
Dependent poor	41.0	41.7	53.7
No income	7.4	4.2	0.6
Total	100.0	100.0%	100.0%
Total (in 1,000s)	(486)	(1,154)	(1,730)

[a] Poverty status defined here as having income below 125% of the official poverty threshold.

[b] Families in poverty defined as *working poor* if more than half of total family income derives from earned income; as *dependent poor* if half or more derives from public assistance.

35

Table 4.5

Percentage of Black Children in Poverty by Age Group and Family Type: 1959-1984, Selected Years

Age of Children and
Family Type (by head)

Children 0-2 years				
Married couple	59.5%	28.5%	20.6%	25.7%
Formerly married woman	85.1	68.7	61.0	65.2
Never-married woman	88.9	75.0	76.4	86.7
Children 3-5 years				
Married couple	59.9	28.6	19.0	24.8
Formerly married woman	86.7	69.0	61.8	60.5
Never-married woman	88.0	77.2	74.0	80.3
Children 6-17 years				
Married couple	58.5	29.3	18.7	20.9
Formerly married woman	82.6	65.6	55.5	60.2
Never-married woman	85.0	73.4	66.1	72.5

Table 4.6

Distribution of Black Related Children Under Age 3 by Family Type and Poverty[a]/Dependency[b] Status: 1969, 1979, 1984

Family Type (by head) and Poverty Status	1969	1979	1984
Married couple			
Not in poverty	59.5%	71.2%	65.4%
Working poor	38.0	25.0	31.3
Dependent poor	2.0	2.8	2.6
No income	0.5	1.0	0.7
Total	99.9%	100.0%	100.0%
Total (in 1,000s)	(893)	(777)	(691)
Formerly married woman			
Not in poverty	21.2%	28.6%	25.7%
Working poor	42.3	40.0	40.4
Dependent poor	31.0	27.9	32.5
No income	5.6	3.5	1.3
Total	100.1%	100.0%	99.9%
Total (in 1,000s)	(300)	(351)	(417)
Never-married woman			
Not in poverty	17.3%	17.2%	11.5%
Working poor	30.1	28.5	25.3
Dependent poor	43.5	49.1	63.2
No income	9.1	5.2	0.0
Total	100.0%	100.0%	100.0%
Total (in 1,000s)	(108)	(265)	(389)

[a] Poverty status defined here as having income below 125% of the official poverty threshold.

[b] Families in poverty defined as *working poor* if more than half of total family income derives from earned income; as *dependent poor* if half or more derives from public assistance.

5
The Impact of Family Structure on Income

Because the economic well-being of children depends on that of their families, this chapter looks in detail at how black families of different types were faring economically between 1959 and 1984. The data show that black families of all types experienced a real decline in their economic status at some point during this period—a decline that appears to have contributed even more significantly than changing family structure to the growing impoverishment of black children. However, female-headed families faced greater economic adversity than two-parent families. As expected, the research uncovered a growing economic disparity between families headed by single women and other family types. As a result, the children of single women are at an even greater disadvantage than children of divorced women or children in two-parent families.

Median and Per-Capita Family Income, by Family Type

Both median and per-capita income for black families (and comparable white families) rose overall between 1959 and 1979 and declined overall between 1979 and 1984.[1] However, for female-headed families—particularly those headed by single women—income growth was much smaller and declines much greater than for married-couple families.

Median Family Income. The median income for households headed by single women, as a proportion of the income of married-couple families, fell from 37 percent in 1959 to only 23 percent in 1984. For families headed by divorced women, the income ratio dropped much less, going from 42 percent in 1959 to 37 percent in 1984.

Figure 5.1
Per-Capita Income* of Black Families by Family Type: 1959, 1969, 1979, 1984

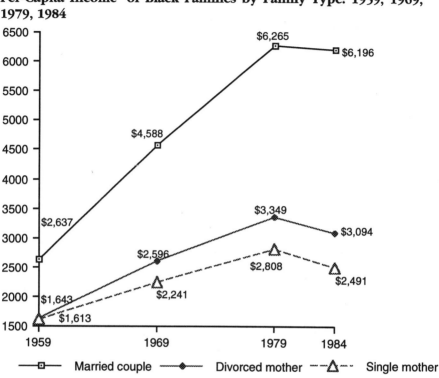

*Figures in constant 1984 dollars

Because divorced women did not suffer as much economically, the median income of families headed by single women also fell during the same period as a proportion of the income of divorcée-headed families, from 87 percent to 62 percent. (For median family income ratios for selected years, see Table 5.1. Actual income figures appear in Table 5.2)

Per-Capita Family Income. Because black (and white) families had fewer children after 1960, when one examines changes in family income it is important to take account of declines in family size. It is possible, for example, to have a decrease in family income without a decrease in per-capita income, if family size shrinks at least as much as income. However, this was not the case throughout the 1960-84 period. Trends in per-capita family income (total family income divided by the number of family members in the household) mirror those for median family income (see Figure 5.1).

From 1959 to 1979, the per-capita income of married-couple families increased sharply, going from $2,637 to $6,265 in constant 1984 dollars. However, divorced mothers and their children did not experience such substantial economic gains, and single mothers did even less well. Although per-capita family income was about the same for all female-headed families in 1959, 20 years later this income figure for single-woman households was only 84 percent what it was for households headed by divorced women ($2,808 and $3,349, respectively).

Although from 1979 to 1984 per-capita income in all family types declined, families headed by single women suffered the largest drop (11.3 percent), followed by those headed by divorced women (7.6 percent) and by married-couple families (1.1 percent). In 1984, the per-capita family income of families headed by single women ($2,491) was only four-fifths that of families headed by divorced women ($3,094) and two-fifths that of two-parent families ($6,196). This represents a substantial change since 1959 when the per-capita family income of families headed by single women ($1,613) was nearly the same as that of families headed by divorced women ($1,643) and three-fifths that of two-parent families ($2,637).

Female-Headed Families: The Growing Income Gap Between Single and Divorced Heads of Household, 1969-1984. The growing economic divergence between families headed by single women and families headed by divorced women is documented by additional indicators, including not only the percentage of each family type that lives in poverty but also the income deficit (the amount needed to bring a family up to the poverty level) for each family type. These data suggest that families headed by single women are increasingly likely to be poor—and that the real income of those families that are poor has plummeted over time.

Percentage of Families in Poverty, by Marital Status

In 1959, about 78 percent of both family types (headed by single mothers and by divorced mothers) were poor. By 1979, this had markedly improved: 62.5 percent of families headed by single

Figure 5.2
**Per-Capita Income Deficit* for Black Female-Headed Families: 1959,
1969, 1979, 1984**

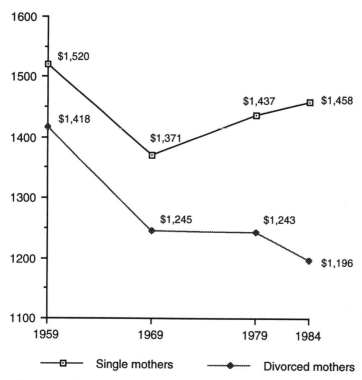

*The income deficit is the amount by which a family income falls below the poverty
line. Per-capita income deficit is the family's deficit amount divided by the total
number of family members.

women were poor compared with 48.7 percent of those headed by
divorced women. By 1984 these figures had risen respectively to
68.5 percent and 52.2 percent, reflecting a renewed decline in
economic status.

The increasing poverty of families headed by single mothers is
related both to the fact that nearly half (46.6 percent) of such families
depended on public assistance in 1984 (see Table 5.3), up from just
over one-third in 1969 (34.9 percent) and in 1979 (36.5 percent), and
to the fact that the real value of public assistance declined after the

mid-1970s. Not surprisingly, the average income of dependent-poor families headed by single women in 1984—$3,922—was far below the poverty line.

By contrast, the percentage of dependent-poor families headed by divorced women rose very little between 1969 and 1984. In 1984, most black families headed by divorced women were either working poor (38.0 percent) or non-poor (37.6 percent). The average income for these families combined was over $12,000.

The Income Deficit, by Marital Status. Changes in families' "income-deficit"—the amount by which a family's income falls below the poverty line—further emphasize the extent to which families headed by single women face even greater poverty than families headed by divorced mothers.

In 1959, the income of all poor female-headed families, on average, was less than two-fifths of their minimum needs (38 percent for those with single heads, 39 percent for those with divorced heads). From 1959 to 1979, income increased to 50 percent (single heads) and 54 percent (divorced heads) of minimum needs, indicating some improvement. By 1984, however, the ratio had once again decreased: to 46 percent (single heads) and 52 percent (divorced heads). All poor female-headed families were in dire need, but poor families with single heads fared worst.

The Per-Capita Income Deficit, by Marital Status. Average family size differs for single and divorced women. Thus, trends in per-capita income deficits (total family income deficit, divided by the number of family members in the household) are significant (see Figure 5.2), and these figures provide additional evidence of the hardship faced by families headed by single women.

In 1959, the per-capita income deficit for families with never-married heads was only slightly larger than that of families with a formerly married head ($1,520, compared with $1,418). By 1984, while the overall or absolute size of the deficits had declined, the gap between them had widened considerably (from $102 to $262).

Table 5.1

Median Family Income Ratios for Black Families with Children: 1959-1984, Selected Years

Ratio of Income of Families Headed by. . .	To Income of Families Headed by. . .	1959	1969	1979	1984
Never-married mothers	Formerly married mothers	.87	.75	.64	.62
Formerly married mothers	Married couples	.42	.42	.39	.37
Never-married mothers	Married couples	.37	.32	.25	.23

Table 5.2

Median Income (in constant 1984 dollars) of Black Families by Family Type: 1959-1984

Family Type (by head)	1959	1969	1979	1984
Married couple	$13,030	$21,649	$27,184	$25,973
Formerly married woman	5,533	9,197	10,707	9,500
Never-married woman	4,819	6,933	6,850	5,893

Table 5.3

Distribution of Black Female-Headed Families With Children by Family Type and Poverty[a]/Dependency[b] Status: 1969, 1979, 1984

Family Type (by head) and Poverty Status	1969	1979	1984
Formerly married woman			
Not in poverty	32.2%	41.6%	37.6%
Working poor	41.4	34.8	38.0
Dependent poor	21.5	20.7	23.5
No income	4.9	2.9	0.9
Total	100.0%	100.0%	100.0%
Total (in 1,000s)	(881)	(1,253)	(1,445)
Never-married woman			
Not in poverty	25.3%	29.8%	25.3%
Working poor	32.7	29.6	27.0
Dependent poor	34.9	36.5	46.6
No income	7.1	4.1	1.1
Total	100.0%	100.0%	100.0%
Total (in 1,000s)	(187)	(558)	(890)

[a] Poverty status defined here as having income below 125% of the official poverty threshold.

[b] Families in poverty defined as *working poor* if more than half of total family income derives from earned income; as *dependent poor* if half or more derives from public assistance.

6
Factors Affecting Family Income

Although female-headed families are more likely to be poor than married-couple families, it is essential to note that families headed by women, especially single mothers, are also more likely to be poor and more likely to face even deeper poverty than formerly. There are several reasons why such families have fared so poorly and why their situation has been worsening. The likely extent to which family income levels between 1959 and 1984 were influenced by changes in four factors—public assistance, number of earners per family, age of family head, and regional economic conditions—is examined next. Each factor is reviewed separately.[1]

Trends in Public Assistance

Welfare regulations that went into effect in 1981 (the Omnibus Budget Reconciliation Act, or OBRA) contributed in several ways to the impoverishment of black families and their children. First, growing numbers of poor children received less income from public assistance because eligibility requirements were tightened and benefit levels were reduced for various welfare programs.[2] Second, those who had been working while also receiving public assistance now had less incentive to do so because the allowable deductions for earnings and work-related expenses were reduced.[3] Third, after 1980, state agencies stepped up their denial of AFDC benefits for procedural reasons (rather than for excess income) by about 75 percent; "in the United States in FY 1985-1986, 60 percent of all eligible denials were due to 'failure to comply with procedural requirements'."[4] Families headed by single women were the hardest hit by changing welfare regulations.

Enrollment Cutbacks During the 1980s. The number of families receiving AFDC was nearly 3.5 times as large in 1980

(3.8 million) as in 1965 (1.1 million).[5] Between 1980 and 1985, however, 100,000 families were removed from the AFDC rolls, probably as a result of changes implemented under OBRA.

Table 6.1 shows changes in the AFDC enrollment of black families from 1969 to 1984.[6] In 1984, 28 percent of all black families with children received AFDC, up from 19.1 percent in 1969.

Female-headed families were much more likely than married-couple families to receive assistance. The percentage of families headed by a never-married woman that received AFDC benefits rose from 50.3 percent in 1969 to 57.2 percent in 1984, whereas the proportion of other family types receiving assistance increased from 1969 to 1979 and then declined to their respective 1969 levels by 1984.

Declining Assistance Levels. While the proportion of poor children grew by 30 percent between the mid-1970s and the mid-1980s, AFDC benefit levels fell about one-third in real dollar value.[7] From 1970 to 1985, monthly AFDC payments for a family of four with no countable income[8] kept pace with or exceeded the rate of inflation in only three states: California, Maine, and Wisconsin.[9] In all family types, the average public assistance income for families receiving AFDC was much lower in 1984 than in 1969, reflecting both the decline in the real value of public assistance income and the effects of OBRA.

Moreover, the ratio of public assistance to total family income changed in similar directions for all family types: declining between 1969 and 1979 and increasing between 1979 and 1984. For both married-couple families and families headed by divorced women, this ratio was about the same in 1984 as in 1969. For black families headed by single women, in contrast, the ratio of AFDC income to total family income was nearly 14 percent higher in 1984 than in 1969.

Divergence in Family Type and Its Effect on Children

The divergence among family types began after 1979 and dramatically affected the economic well-being of black children (compare Tables 4.4 and 6.1, pages 35 and 60). That is, although the ratio of public assistance to total family income increased between 1979 and 1984 in all family types, the economic consequences for children varied considerably by family type. The proportion of dependent-poor children in families headed by single women rose 12 percentage points from 1979 to 1984, while the proportion of dependent-poor children in other family types increased very little or not at all. (Table 4.4.) Thus, while AFDC constituted an increasing proportion of family income for all family types after 1979, the economic effects were much more deleterious for children of single women.

It should be noted that between 1979 and 1984 the percentage of families headed by single women increased, but the proportion of these women and their families who relied on public assistance as their sole source of income changed little: from 53.1 percent in 1979 to 52.3 percent in 1984. However, the proportion of families headed by single women that had income from both public assistance and earnings declined (from 19.6 percent in 1979 to 14.5 percent in 1984), and the proportion whose only source of family income was earnings rose (from 21.2 percent to 25.7 percent). This was likely a result of OBRA.

Implications for Black Child Poverty

Reductions in, and losses of, AFDC income, particularly in families headed by single women, have certainly taken their toll on the economic well-being of black children and their families. However, the findings reported here indicate that other factors besides AFDC have contributed to the declining economic status of families headed by never-married women.

For instance, as we have seen, while the same proportion of these families relied exclusively on public assistance in both 1979 and 1984, the percentage who relied on both public assistance and earnings declined. At the same time, the ratio of public assistance to total family income was much higher in 1984 than in 1979 for single-woman families, and given the weakening of assistance benefits, this means their total incomes were severely limited.

Moreover, poor black families headed by single women were increasingly likely to rely exclusively on earnings. Because of the increased reliance on earnings rather than on AFDC income, it seems probable that the economic well-being of many of these families was more adversely affected by the decline in real earnings than by a decline in real AFDC income.

49

Trends in the Number of Earners per Family

Two trends have lowered the number of earners in female-headed families (especially those headed by single women) relative to the number of earners in married-couple families: (1) changes in the comparative employment rates for married and unmarried black mothers and (2) changes in the proportion of black families with related adults living in the household.[10]

Trends in Employment Rates, by Family Type. The rapid growth in employment for both black and white married women after 1960 has been well documented.[11] The present analysis shows that from 1960 to 1985, the percentage of married black mothers who were employed nearly doubled, going from 35 percent in 1960 to 64.6 percent in 1985. In contrast, employment rates for unmarried black mothers rose only slightly: the percentage of divorced family heads in the work force increased from 47.9 percent in 1960 to 54.1 percent in 1980 and then declined to 50.6 percent by 1985; the percentage of single mothers who were employed increased slightly from 1960 to 1970 (41.8 percent to 44.5 percent) and then dropped back to its 1960 level (41.9 percent in 1985). Thus, while married black mothers were less likely to work than unmarried black mothers in 1960, they were much more likely to work by 1985.

Changes in Family Composition, by Family Type. Qualitative studies[12] suggest that extended families can provide a social support system that facilitates the employment of married women or female family heads (for example, extended families can take over some of the household's domestic responsibilities or contribute directly to family income, or both). As already noted, however, female-headed families (and particularly families headed by single women) have become increasingly less likely than married-couple families to include adult relatives. As Table 6.3 shows, in 1984 nearly three-fourths of married-couple families included at least two earners, compared with nearly one-fourth of families headed by divorced women and fewer than one-tenth of families headed by single women. In contrast, 42.5 percent of families headed by single women and 28.9 percent of families headed by divorced women had no earners in the family. Only 4.3 percent of married-couple families were in a comparable situation.

Implications for Black Child Poverty. While changes in the number of earners per family have clearly affected the economic status of children in each family type, the actual impact is not entirely certain. From 1959 to 1969, for instance, child poverty declined substantially among black children with single mothers, even though employment rates for these same family heads increased only slightly and the proportion of such families with related adults actually declined by nearly 50 percent.

From 1969 to 1979, the proportion of single mothers who were employed declined imperceptibly, as did the proportion of these families that included other adult relatives. Yet child poverty actually declined (Figure 4.1) and per-capita income increased (Figure 5.1) for these families. It is doubtful that public assistance is a factor here, since the percentage of these families that received assistance changed little and the real value of public assistance income dropped during this period (see Table 6.1). Apparently, more subtle factors determine a family's earning capacity and the likelihood that a family (including its children) is poor.

Changes in Regional Economic Conditions

A family's income (and its poverty status) significantly depends on its geographic location, as suggested in chapter two. Shifts in the regional employment picture during the 1970s enabled Southern families to improve their economic status, while families in other regions were losing ground.

During the 1970s, employment for black males fell more than twice as much in Northern cities as in Southern cities, and unemployment rates for black males increased by about 60 percent more in the North than in the South. Employment for black females during the same period increased in most SMSAs, but the gains were much greater in the South. On average, real median family income increased by $1,285 in Southern metropolitan areas but declined by $804 in Northern SMSAs.

From 1979 to 1984, poverty rates continued to rise for most families in Northeastern and Midwestern urban areas and to fall slightly for many families in Southern metropolitan areas (see Table 6.2). Although the Northeast did experience economic growth following the 1981-1982 recession, black families in that region apparently did not benefit fully; all family types had higher poverty rates in 1984 than in 1979. At the same time, rural areas in all regions

51

continued to see a drop in employment and earnings.[13]

Regional Trends in Family Economic Status. Not all families were affected equally by these regional economic changes. Families headed by single women, in particular, experienced more persistent poverty than other family types, not only in regions whose economy was in decline but in areas of economic growth as well. In the urban South, for example, their poverty rates declined only marginally compared to much larger decreases in poverty experienced by other family types. Finally, compared with other family types, families headed by single women living in areas of economic decline increased substantially as a proportion of all families, whereas families headed by single women living in areas of economic growth increased only modestly as a proportion of all families.

Implications for black child poverty. While geographic location is associated with change in the economic status of black children, location does not appear to be an independent cause of differences in child poverty rates by family type. However, geographic location in conjunction with age of the family head apparently has influenced the relative well-being of children in different family types.

The Growing Link Between Age of Family Head and Family Economic Status

Between 1960 and 1985, family economic status came to be more closely linked to the age of the family head, with families whose heads were older being better off than other families. Young black families were much more likely to be poor in 1984 than 1979, regardless of family structure. Older families, in contrast—including those headed by single women—were neither more nor less likely to be poor in 1984.

How Age is Related to Economic Status. Older workers with more job experience normally have higher incomes than newer entrants into the labor force. However, three recent trends in labor force status and earnings have tended to widen the economic differential between younger and older workers even more than might be expected[14]:

(1) Rising unemployment among black men in their 20s: Unemployment is high among young black men and has increased over the last 20 years. The deterioration in the labor force status of black

men is even starker when one focuses on employment rates rather than labor force participation rates (which include the unemployed known to be looking for work).[15] From the mid-1970s to the mid-1980s, the percentage of black men in their 20s who were employed year-round declined by one-third (going from 48.3 percent to 32.3 percent), while the comparable percentage for young white men changed little (from 49.7 percent to 50.7 percent).[16] In contrast, the percentage of women in their 20s who were year-round workers increased, especially among whites.

(2) Declining real earnings for workers in their 20s: Except for young white women, all workers in their 20s have seen their real annual earnings decline since the mid-1970s.[17] Explanations include the baby boomers' entry into the labor market,[18] shifts in industrial employment from manufacturing to trades and services,[19] and shifts in the employment of young workers within industries and firms.[20]

(3) Declining real earnings for young workers with no college education: The decline in real earnings since the mid-1970s has been steepest for high school dropouts and high school graduates in their 20s. From the mid-1970s to the mid-1980s, among 20- to 24-year-old high school graduates with no college education, real earnings fell by 26.1 percent for white men, 52.2 percent for black men, and 40.8 percent for black women.[21] Real annual earnings also declined among 25- to 29-year-olds with no college education. As a result, between 1973 and 1985, the annual-earnings advantages of college-educated males (25 to 29 years old) relative to high school dropouts in the same age group rose from 57 percent to 132 percent.[22]

Age of Family Head and Family Type. Given the especially precarious circumstances of young families, it is not surprising that these families were becoming economically worse off than older families between 1979 and 1984. As Figure 6.1 shows, for example, family income of young two-parent families declined 5 percentage points in comparison with family income of older two-parent families (from 79.2 percent to 74.2 percent). Comparable statistics for families headed by divorced women reflect the same pattern.

Further, per-capita income was lower for young families of all family types in 1984 than in 1979 (See Figure 6.2). While change in per-capita income was modest for families headed by divorced women, the declines were more dramatic for two-parent families (a

53

Figure 6.1
**Relative Income (Ratio*) of Younger Black Families Compared to
Older Black Families, by Family Type: 1979 and 1984**

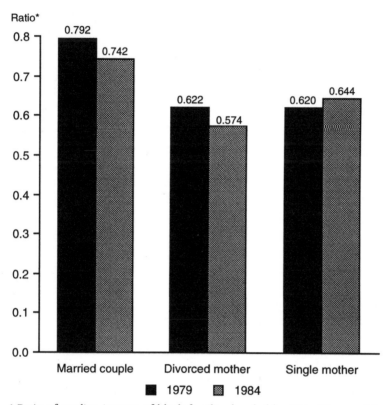

* Ratio of median income of black families headed by 20-to-29-year-olds to that of
black families with heads age 30 or over.

12 percentage point drop) and for families headed by single women
(a 22-point drop).

Declines in the median and per-capita income of young black
families meant that the proportion of these families that are poor was
growing in comparison with older families. Figure 6.3 shows that
from 1979 to 1984 poverty rates increased in all family types when
the head was 20 to 29 years old. These data are consistent with
trends in the labor force participation rate of black males and in the
real earnings of black men and women in their 20s, as well as with

Figure 6.2
Relative Per-Capita Income (Ratio*) of Younger Black Families Compared to Older Black Families, by Family Type: 1979 and 1984

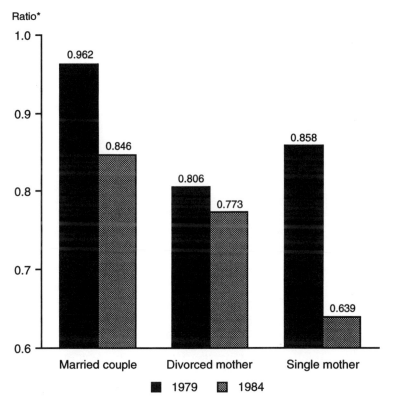

* Ratio of median per-capita income of black families headed by 20-to-29-year-olds to that of black families with heads age 30 or over.

changes in the real value of public assistance. In contrast, poverty rates changed little if the family head was over 30, except for families headed by divorced women.

The Growing Vulnerability of Single Mothers

Age-related factors compound the economic hardships faced by single mothers, in particular, because these women are more likely to be concentrated in the hardest-hit age bracket. Young mothers are also more likely to have lower per-capita family income, to have

55

lower educational and employment status, and to be concentrated in geographic areas of economic decline.

By 1985, 57.5 percent of all single mothers were in their 20s, the hardest-hit age bracket, compared with 25.4 percent of married women, and 14.3 percent of divorced women. In fact, for each year of data analyzed (see Table 6.4), the proportion of single mothers in their 20s was much larger than the proportion of young mothers in other family categories.

Declining Per-Capita Family Incomes for Young Single Mothers. While per-capita income was lower for young families of all types in 1984 than in 1979 (see Figure 6.2), the decline was most dramatic for families headed by single women because changes in family size for older mothers were very different from changes for younger mothers. In 1979, the mean number of black children in families headed by single women ages 20 to 29 was 1.92, compared with 2.33 for black children in families headed by single women age 30 or older. But in 1984, the mean number of black children was 1.95 for single mothers in both age groups. Even with the slight increase in relative median family income for families headed by 20- to 29-year-olds (Figure 6.1), the shrinking family size of older single women produced the dramatic drop in the relative per-capita incomes of young single mothers.

The Increasing Concentration of Single Mothers Among the Young. In 1969, black families headed by single women in their 20s and 30s were about equally likely to be poor. But by 1984, 78.1 percent of black families headed by single women in their 20s were poor, compared with 53.3 percent of black families headed by single women aged 30 or older. The relative poverty trends for these families accord with their per-capita income trends as shown in Figure 6.2.

At the same time, poverty rates were diverging for young female-headed families (see Figure 6.3), with single women faring worse than divorced women. In 1969, black families headed by single and divorced women in their 20s were about equally likely to be poor. But by 1984, 78.1 percent of young single women were poor, compared with 65.2 percent of young divorced women.

What accounts for the difference in economic well-being between families headed by single and by divorced women in their

Figure 6.3
Percentage of Black Families in Poverty, by Family Type and Age of Head: 1969, 1979, 1984

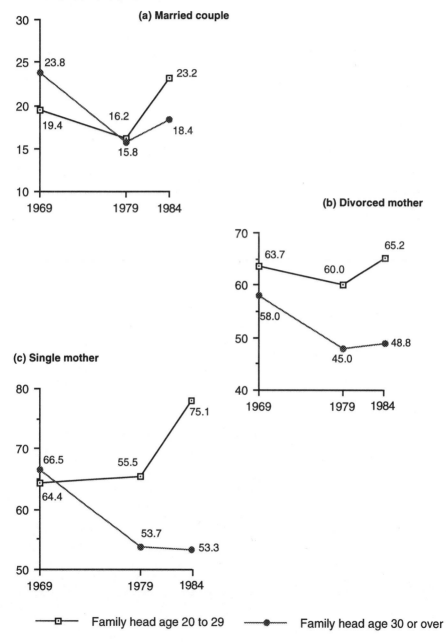

20s? First, the age composition of each group is important. The data show that more single than divorced mothers were in their early 20s (ages 20 to 24), the most economically disadvantaged age bracket. Female heads in their early 20s were almost equally likely to be poor, whether single or divorced (73 and 71 percent, respectively, in 1979; 81 and 82 percent, respectively, by 1984). However, in 1984 the proportion of all single mothers who were 20 to 24 was nearly double the proportion of divorced mothers in that age bracket (44.4 and 23 percent, respectively). If this had not been the case, that is, if single and divorced mothers had been equally likely to be in their early 20s, then 70 percent of families headed by divorced women aged 20 to 29 would have been poor, rather than the actual 65.2 percent.

Second, among female family heads ages 25 to 29, single mothers have been faring worse than divorced mothers. In 1979, 59.9 percent of families headed by single women were poor, compared with 56.6 percent of families headed by divorced women in this same age group. By 1984, the two figures had drifted much further apart: 75.4 percent (single heads) versus 60.0 percent (divorced heads).

Finally, the growing divergence between the two family types is probably related to changes in education and employment among black female heads in their middle to late twenties. From 1980 to 1985, the educational level of black divorced heads increased (with 32.2 percent completing one or more years of college in 1985, up from 24.5 percent in 1980), while the education attainment of single heads changed little (with the proportion completing some college education declining from 21.2 to 18.1 percent). In addition, while the proportion of black female family heads who were employed declined nearly 8 percent among divorced women (from 55.3 to 51.0 percent), it fell by more than 21 percent for single women (from 44.6 to 35.2 percent).

The Concentration of Young Single Mothers in Economically Depressed Regions. The plight of families headed by single women has been exacerbated by the high proportion who live in economically depressed areas, combined with the high percentage who are in their 20s. Urban Northeastern and Midwestern families of all types were more likely to be poor in 1984 than in either 1979 or

1969. However, black families headed by single women are more highly concentrated than other family types in these depressed areas. This trend seems most closely associated with the sharp drop in employment for young black males in the Northeast and Midwest (see chapter two). While marriage rates among all young blacks have declined, these rates are especially low in areas with the fewest employment prospects for black men.[23]

Looking at black families headed by individuals in their 20s across family types, one sees that in 1985, 52 percent of single women lived in the most economically depressed areas (the Midwest and Northeast), compared with only 23.5 percent of married-couple families in this age group (see Table 6.5). Among older black families (those with a head age 30 or older), 48.6 percent of all families headed by never-married women lived in these depressed areas, compared with 35.1 percent of those headed by married couples.

Moreover, many more single mothers than other heads of families were in their 20s. It is therefore enlightening but distressing to examine the effects of geographic location and age of family head simultaneously. In about 30 percent of all black families headed by single women in 1985, the head was 20 to 29 years old and the family lived in the Northeast or Midwest.[23] By contrast, only 6 percent of married-couple families and 6 percent of families headed by a formerly married woman were characterized by these dual handicaps.

Table 6.1

Distribution and Amounts of Public Assistance Income (in constant 1984 dollars) Received by Black Families With Children: 1969, 1979, 1984

	1969	1979	1984
All recipient families			
Number of families (in 1,000s)	6,231	10,703	12,460
Percent of all black families	19.1	25.8	28.0
Married-couple recipient families			
Number of families (in 1,000s)	1,824	2,573	1,625
Percent of all married-couple families	8.8%	12.0%	8.4%
Average assistance income	$3,693	$3,745	$2,792
AFDC income as percent of total family income	19.9%	16.2%	18.9%
Recipient families headed by a formerly-married woman			
Number of families (in 1,000s)	3,468	5,185	5,746
Percent of all formerly-married woman families	39.4%	41.4%	39.7%
Average assistance income	$4,669	$4,148	$3,496
AFDC income as percent of total family income	46.7%	35.9%	46.6%
Recipient families headed by a never-married woman			
Number of families (in 1,000s)	939	2,945	5,089
Percent of all never-married woman families	50.3%	52.7%	57.2%
Average assistance income	$4,715	$3,990	$3,292
AFDC income as a percent of total family income	59.3%	55.0%	67.4%

Table 6.2

Poverty Rates of Black Families With Children by Family Type, Region, and Metro/Nonmetro Area: 1969, 1979, 1984

Family Type (by head)	1969	1979	1984
Married couple			
Northeast metro	11.0%	11.5%	13.3%
Midwest metro	9.6	10.4	14.3
South metro	20.7	13.8	13.1
South nonmetro	42.5	26.0	27.8
West metro	12.8	10.3	16.2
Formerly married woman			
Northeast metro	47.0	45.8	49.9
Midwest metro	50.8	46.2	55.9
South metro	60.8	48.0	46.5
South nonmetro	71.9	60.0	60.4
West metro	51.6	54.0	57.5
Never-married woman			
Northeast metro	56.1	62.7	65.4
Midwest metro	61.9	63.9	74.0
South metro	65.4	60.3	62.2
South nonmetro	83.5	70.1	79.7
West metro	53.5	40.5	45.5

Table 6.3

Distribution of Black Families With Children by Number of Earners in Household and by Family Type: 1979 and 1984

	1979 Family Type (by head)			1984 Family Type (by head)		
Number of Earners	Married Couple	Formerly Married Woman	Never-Married Woman	Married Couple	Formerly Married Woman	Never-Married Woman
None	4.2%	27.0%	40.8%	4.3%	28.9%	42.5%
One	24.5	48.4	48.3	21.6	48.4	48.9
Two or more	71.3	24.6	10.9	74.1	22.7	8.6
Total	100.0%	100.0%	100.0%	100.0%	100.0%	100.0%
Total (1,000s)	(21,457)	(12,534)	(5,585)	(19,339)	(14,453)	(8,901)

Table 6.4

Distribution of Black Families with Children by Family Type and Age of Family Head: 1970, 1980, 1985

	Age 20-29			Age 30 or Older		
Family Type (by head)	1970	1980	1985	1970	1980	1985
Married couple	27.9%	28.0%	25.4%	69.4%	70.8%	74.4%
Formerly married woman	20.0	18.2	14.3	79.3	81.5	85.6
Never-married woman	47.1	57.4	57.5	47.6	38.4	40.4

Table 6.5

Distribution of Black Families with Children by Family Type, Age of Family Head, and Region and Metro/Nonmetro Area: 1985

Family Type (by head)	Age 20-29	Age 30 or Older
Married couple		
Northeast metro	10.0%	19.3%
Midwest metro	13.5	15.8
South metro	38.0	34.6
South nonmetro	28.9	23.2
West metro	9.6	7.1
Total	100.0%	100.0%
Total (in 1,000s)	(473)	(1,389)
Formerly married woman		
Northeast metro	15.9%	18.5%
Midwest metro	23.2	21.9
South metro	37.3	31.0
South nonmetro	17.1	22.1
West metro	6.6	6.4
Total	99.9%	99.9%
Total (in 1,000s)	(202)	(1,197)
Never-married woman		
Northeast metro	26.9%	30.2%
Midwest metro	25.1	18.4
South metro	27.2	25.8
South nonmetro	15.0	18.1
West metro	5.8	7.5
Total	100.0%	100.0%
Total (in 1,000s)	(491)	(349)

63

7

The Growing Vulnerability of Black Children: Policy Implications

The increasing poverty among black children is commonly associated with changes in family structure that have taken place since 1960—more specifically, with the dramatic increase in the number of female-headed families. Because black child poverty has been rising at the same time that family structure has been changing, it is widely assumed that the latter is the cause of the former.

As this study has shown, changing family structure certainly has contributed to the growing impoverishment of black children. A majority of these children now live in female-headed families whose income levels are typically much lower than those of two-parent families. However, changes in the economic conditions faced by many families, regardless of family structure, seem to have played an even greater role in the worsening economic status of black children. In short, the changing economic situations faced by family heads in different age groups, by family heads in different regions, and by single versus divorced mothers have combined to exacerbate the severe economic hardship faced by black children.

A review of the factors that contribute to this economic hardship suggests strategies that might alleviate the conditions in which black children are growing up. While a complete policy prescription is beyond the scope of this monograph, several policy options are discussed at the conclusion of this chapter.

The Growing Vulnerability of Black Children in Young Families

Since the mid-1970s, young blacks (those in their 20s) have suffered sharp declines in employment and earnings. As a result, a rapidly growing number of black children who live in young families are poor in comparison with children in older families. In 1969 the poverty rates of black children did not vary in relation to the age of the family head; by 1984, children in young families were twice as likely to be poor as children in older families. Table 7.1 documents this divergence. Moreover, although a majority of black children live with parents over 30, the percentage with parents in their 20s has increased gradually, from 23.8 percent in 1970 to 27.3 percent in 1985.[1]

In addition, about 2.5 times as many black children in families with parents in their 20s were dependent-poor in 1984 (33.1 percent) as in 1969 (13.4 percent). The increasing proportion of dependent-poor black children in young families corresponded with the decline in the proportion of non-poor children. In contrast, among older families the proportion of non-poor black children increased sharply, as a declining number of the children in these families were either dependent poor or working poor.

The Growing Vulnerability of Black Children With Young Single Mothers. While black children with single mothers are more likely to be poor than are black children in other family types, it is essential to note that these children are also more likely to be poor than they used to be. A major reason for this trend is that an increasing number of black children live with a single mother who is in her 20s, in relation to children in other family types. In 1985, 58.9 percent of all children in families headed by a single woman, compared with 24.3 percent of children in married-couple families and 14.5 percent of children in families headed by a divorced woman, lived with a head aged 20 to 29. Because blacks in their 20s have experienced sharp declines in employment and earnings since the mid-1970s, the worsening hardships of black children in young families was especially pronounced for those with single mothers.

The Changing Poverty Status of Children With Young Single Mothers. Because a growing proportion of never-married heads are in their 20s, black children who live with young mothers in this category are increasingly likely to be poor in comparison with children in other families. Table 7.2 shows trends in the poverty status of black children, broken down by family type and by age of family head.

In most years, children in families headed by single women were more likely to be poor than children in families headed by divorced mothers. When the age of the family head is taken into account, family type has an even greater impact on poverty status.

As Table 4.4 in chapter four indicates, the proportion of black children in 1984 who lived below 125 percent of the poverty line was 12 percentage points higher for those in families headed by single women than for those in families headed by divorced women. Table 7.2 reveals that the difference in poverty rates for these two family types is much smaller if you compare them within age category, being 5.6 percentage points for black children in young families and 5.4 percentage points for children in older families. Thus, if the age distribution of single and divorced female family heads had been the same, the proportion of poor black children would be only about 5 to 6 percentage points higher for those in families with a single mother—rather than the actual 12 percentage point difference.

Growing Welfare Dependency Among Black Children—The Combined Effects of Mothers' Age and Their Concentration in Economically Depressed Areas. In 1985, about 30 percent of all single mothers were in their 20s and lived in the urban Northeast and Midwest; by comparison, only 6 percent of divorced mothers were in their 20s and lived in these two regions. The Northeast and Midwest have experienced economic stagnation and decline since 1970, especially compared to the urban South.

Residential location, in conjunction with the relative youth of single-female family heads, has also affected the proportion of children in families dependent on public assistance. The aggregate data used in Table 4.4 show that the proportion of dependent-poor black children in families headed by single women increased from 1979 to 1984. However, the proportion of dependent-poor black children in such families increased very little in the South. For those who lived outside the South, the increase in the proportion of dependent-poor children was dramatic: a 13.8 percentage point increase in the urban Northeast and a 23.3 percentage point increase in the urban Midwest.

67

Figure 7.1
Percentage of All Black Children Under Age Three in Families Headed by a 20- to 29-Year-Old, by Family Type: 1970, 1980, 1985

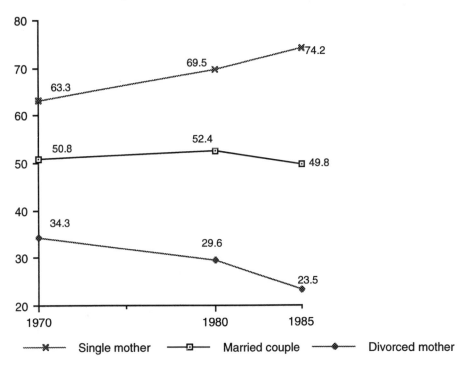

Thus, in 1984 the percentage of dependent-poor children in families headed by a single black mother was 36.2 percent for those living in Southern urban areas, 63.8 percent for those living in Northeastern urban areas, and 72.2 percent for those in Midwestern urban areas (whereas the nationwide figure for 1984 was 53.7 percent, as shown in Table 4.4).

Declining Economic Status of Black Children Under Age Three With Young Single Mothers. The findings reported here suggest that these combined factors of residential location and age of family head have strongly influenced the economic status of black children in different family types. Moreover, it is the very youngest children, those under the age of three, who have been most severely affected by these combined factors. Very young children who live with single mothers have fared the worst of all because, as Figure 7.1 shows, they are increasingly concentrated in families headed by a woman who is in her 20s.

The Likely Permanence of Childhood Poverty

If recent trends in poverty for single mothers continue, a growing percentage of black children will experience severe economic hardship throughout their childhood.

The living arrangements of many black children born to unmarried women tend to be permanent, since these women appear unlikely to marry at any point in their lives.[2] Hofferth (1985) estimates that black children born to never-married mothers in 1980 could expect to spend three-fourths of their entire childhood in one-parent families.

Moreover, black children who spend their entire childhood with a mother who never marries can expect to be poor for most of those years. Based on estimates derived from the 1980 Census data used in this study, these children could expect to spend about 15 of their 17 childhood years in poverty.[3]

This finding accords with data showing that the economic status of 20- to 24-year-old single mothers does not appear to improve as they grow older, especially when compared with divorced family heads. While 73 percent of all single mothers lived in poverty when they were 20 to 24 years old (in 1979), 75.4 percent of them were poor when they were 25 to 29 years old (in 1984). In contrast, 71 percent of divorced mothers were impoverished when they were 20 to 24 years old (in 1979), but only 60 percent of this group still lived in poverty when they were 25 to 29 years old (in 1984). If these trends continue, not only will a growing proportion of black children be born poor but, in the absence of some significant intervention, many of them will never escape poverty.

Implementing Policies to Save America's Children

This study has documented the declining economic status of black children and has identified several factors that have contributed to growing poverty among this population. While the situation for black children and their families is the most dramatic, in some ways their plight is merely a magnification of the problems faced by many young families in the United States. Therefore, even though strategies must be carefully crafted to ensure that they are targeted toward the most needy, policies designed to alleviate the conditions in which black children live will provide direct and indirect benefits to others in American society.

Short-Term Strategies. Growing and persistent poverty has short-run and long-run consequences. In the very short run, lack of income affects a child's living conditions—availability of adequate food and shelter, access to health care, education, and so on. Deprivation in any or all of these basic areas can affect a child's physical and social development and have an impact on future economic circumstances. Part of a strategy to improve conditions for black children must include ways of increasing family income immediately.

Policies that have the most immediate impact on family income are those that involve income transfers. One approach is to increase AFDC benefit levels and expand eligibility. This seems unlikely to gain much political support, since seven states and the District of Columbia cut benefit levels in 1992, and nine states have tightened eligibility requirements.[4] As indicated earlier in this study, the real value of public assistance benefits has declined since 1975, leaving families that are solely dependent on public assistance with ever larger poverty deficits. The only major offsetting change in the program has been the extension of AFDC eligibility for two-parent families (where both parents are unemployed) to all 50 states, which took place under the Family Support Act of 1988. In most states, however, eligibility is restricted to very short periods of time and the change has no impact on single-parent families.

A more politically feasible approach to increasing family income in the black community is a more universal program that guarantees minimum support to all children. The United States is one of the few industrialized countries that does not have some type of child allowance program. A recently completed Joint Center study of poverty and economic change in eight industrialized countries shows that the limited public support given to families with children was a more important factor in growing poverty in the United States during the 1980s than slow economic growth.[5] In fact, the United States fared better in terms of economic growth than most of the other countries studied, but its taxes and transfer policies did far less to lift families out of poverty than did the policies of the majority of the other countries included in the analysis.

In the past few years, two versions of a child support strategy have been put forth for consideration by the federal government. One is the universal child tax credit, which could be integrated into the existing tax structure, thus making it relatively inexpensive to administer. A $1,000 credit (per child) was recommended by the National Commission on Children in 1991 and was subsequently considered by the U.S. Congress.[6] In order for a child tax credit to benefit children in poverty, it must be refundable (as recommended by the Commission). If it is not refundable, it will have limited benefits for children in families whose tax liability is less than the size of the credit. It will also have little or no benefit for children in families on public assistance if program benefits are reduced as a result of the implementation of the refundable child credit.

Another type of child allowance that has been proposed is the assured (insured) child benefit. This proposal would establish guaranteed payment for children in single-parent families. It would combine a more vigorous child support enforcement program with a guaranteed level of benefit. If payment from the absent parent was below the guarantee, the government would make up the difference, thereby assuring an economic floor for all children.

At this point, neither child allowance proposal is likely to pass the Congress, but their inclusion in future legislation is highly probable.

Medium-Range Strategies. Providing cash support to families, while essential in the short run, is not a strategy designed to promote economic independence. Moreover, it is unlikely that any child allowance program will provide more than minimal economic support. This study has reinforced findings from other studies on the deteriorating economic circumstances faced by young families. Workers without any college education who have entered the labor force in the past 15 years have faced more limited economic opportunities than their parents. The key to economic advancement is better training for young people, both those heading families today and those who are likely to become parents in the near future.

A first step toward the development of a national training initiative for young parents was embodied in the Job Opportunity and Basic Skills (JOBS) Training portion of the Family Support Act. The objective of this program is to reduce long-term dependence on public assistance by bolstering the education and job skills of parents in the AFDC program. Priority groups include young mothers and those without a high school education, two groups found more likely to be long-term recipients of welfare benefits. Evaluation of demonstration programs and state initiatives of the 1980s that have similar features have found them to produce modest increases in individual earnings and family incomes.[7] It appears that a fully implemented JOBS program would have the potential for improving the economic conditions in which a substantial proportion of black children live. Most states have reported, however, that they expect to have difficulties implementing the JOBS program.[8]

Moreover, recent research suggests that even fully implemented programs are unlikely to move many families above the poverty line. Poor economic conditions in most states are likely to hinder the success of the JOBS program. Three-fourths of all states have indicated that the number of JOBS participants exceeds the number of employment opportunities throughout the state.[9]

Further, the results of a recent study,[10] which examined whether young single mothers could be expected to earn their way out of poverty without public assistance, were far from promising. Many of these mothers would remain near or below the poverty line even if they were employed full-time, because most of them who work are employed in minimum-wage jobs. Even if the JOBS program could considerably increase the earnings capacity of single mothers employed at full-time, minimum-wage jobs, a young single mother with two children would need a wage increase of about $3.37 per hour (in 1989 dollars) to reach the poverty line without public assistance.[11] This would mean an increase in earnings of nearly $6,000 per year ($3.37 x 1,750 hours of work per year). A wage increase of this magnitude is an unlikely outcome of the JOBS program since the average increase in yearly earnings in previous job-training programs has usually ranged from very little change up to $1,500 per year.[12]

While increasing attention has been devoted to improving the employability of young mothers (even though sufficient resources have not been provided), far less attention has been given to increasing the job skills of young males who are likely to be the fathers of black children. This may be partially due to the fact that many of the programs in place over the past 20 years have been less successful at increasing the employment and earnings of young men than they have been at improving the earned income of young disadvantaged women. But growing joblessness among young black males and the role that this seems to be playing in reduced family formation suggest that this area can no longer be ignored. Programs that improve school-to-work transitions, provide job-related skills, and reduce young men's likelihood of being drawn into the illegal economy are long overdue. However, these strategies are unlikely to be successful without a growth in the number of jobs available to non-college youth. Several promising initiatives are currently under discussion, but it is too soon to determine if they will have a significant impact on the economic situation of young males.

Long-Term Strategies. There is growing evidence that the poverty faced by black children is becoming an intergenerational phenomenon. Adolescents who had few incentives for postponing parenting are the parents of a significant proportion of the poorest black children. Although many children who grow up in the bleakest of circumstances are able to overcome the barriers they face and achieve success, a large number do not.

One of the keys to a successful future is a good basic education. Mastery of basic skills is essential for entry into higher education and, increasingly, for entry into the labor force after high school. Large urban school districts are not currently meeting the needs of black children; indeed, they seem to be failing a substantial proportion of the school-age population regardless of race or income level. The inadequacy of resources is but one cause of the shortcomings of American schools. New strategies for structuring schools and instilling learning should be among the major ingredients in any program for strengthening the next generation.

The educational system is not the only institution that needs to be examined, revitalized, and strengthened. As this study has shown, the extended family that sustained the black community for generations is increasingly unavailable to children in single-parent families. This has consequences far beyond the reduction in household income. Children who grow up in single-parent families without other adults in the household are more likely to drop out of school, to marry or become parents early, and to engage in various forms of antisocial behavior.[13]

While one long-term strategy may be to restore absent parents to the family, a short-term strategy that would have a long-term impact would be to develop ways of replacing the extended family. Community-based initiatives, such as mentoring and related activities, seek to do that. While there is little systematic evidence to suggest that existing programs of this nature have a significant impact on outcomes for at-risk children, this is an avenue that must be explored in greater detail.

Concluding Comments

Thirty years ago, the black community was entering a period of economic and social advancement. Buoyed by the vigorous economic expansion of the 1960s and the implementation of numerous social and civil rights programs, blacks were able to increase their educational levels and improve their economic status. Many were able to leave inner-city neighborhoods behind and join their white counterparts in the suburbs. Despite these gains, poverty and despair are growing within the black community. The challenge that the black community and the larger society now face is how to improve the situation of the next generation of children in a much less expansive economic era.

Table 7.1

Distribution of Black Children by Age of Family Head and Poverty[a]/ Dependency[b] Status: 1969, 1979, 1984

Age of Family Head and Poverty Status	1969	1979	1984
Age 20-29			
Not in poverty	47.6%	48.2%	34.9%
Working poor	36.1	28.9	31.5
Dependent poor	13.4	20.2	33.1
No income	2.9	2.6	0.5
Total	100.0%	99.9%	100.0%
Total (in 1,000s)	(2,169)	(2,423)	(2,486)
Age 30 or older			
Not in poverty	46.5%	55.8%	70.4%
Working poor	40.9	30.0	27.3
Dependent poor	10.6	12.6	2.1
No income	2.0	1.6	0.2
Total	100.0%	100.0%	100.0%
Total (in 1,000s)	(6,933)	(6,722)	(6,615)

[a] Poverty defined here as having income below 125% of the official poverty threshold.

[b] Families in poverty defined as *working poor* if more than half of total family income derives from earned income; as *dependent poor* if half or more derives from public assistance.

Table 7.2

Distribution of Black Children by Family Type, Age of Family Head, and Poverty[a]/Dependency[b] Status: 1969, 1979, 1984

Family Type: By Head, Age of Head, and Poverty Status	1969	1979	1984
Married couple			
Age 20-29			
Not in poverty	61.3%	72.0%	67.2%
Working poor	36.7	24.8	29.9
Dependent poor	1.6	2.4	2.9
No income	0.4	0.8	0.0
Total	100.0%	100.0%	100.0%
Total (in 1,000s)	(1,435)	(1,221)	(962)
Age 30 or older			
Not in poverty	58.4%	74.5%	70.4%
Working poor	38.6	23.3	27.3
Dependent poor	2.5	2.5	2.1
No income	0.5	0.7	0.2
Total	100.0%	100.0%	100.0%
Total (in 1000s)	(5816)	(3523)	(2998)
Formerly-married woman			
Age 20-29			
Not in poverty	18.7%	24.8%	17.6%
Working poor	37.4	36.9	42.7
Dependent poor	35.9	33.7	37.6
No income	8.0	4.5	2.1
Total	100.0%	99.9%	100.0%
Total (in 1,000s)	(483)	(510)	(449)

Table 7.2 (cont'd.)

Age 30 or older			
Not in poverty	24.8%	35.1%	32.1%
Working poor	45.9	39.0	39.1
Dependent poor	24.8	23.3	28.1
No income	4.5	2.6	0.6
Total	100.0%	100.0%	99.9 %
Total (in 1,000s)	(2,068)	(2,491)	(2,640)
Never-married woman			
Age 20-29			
Not in poverty	18.1%	19.5%	12.1%
Working poor	28.1	29.3	25.4
Dependent poor	46.0	46.3	62.1
No income	0.4	4.8	0.4
Total	100.0%	99.9%	100.0%
Total (in 1,000s)	(199)	(614)	(997)
Age 30 or older			
Not in poverty	17.9%	28.3%	26.7%
Working poor	38.5	33.6	30.8
Dependent poor	38.4	35.0	41.7
No income	5.2	3.0	0.8
Total	100.0%	99.9%	100.0%
Total (in 1,000s)	(264)	(500)	(702)

[a] Poverty defined here as having income below 125% of the official poverty threshold.

[b] Families in poverty defined as *working poor* if more than half of total family income derives from earned income; as *dependent poor* if half or more derives from public assistance.

NOTES

Chapter 1: Introduction

1. This same assumption has also been called into question by Bane (1986), who reports that over half (55%) of the black-white poverty gap is due to "higher poverty rates for blacks within household composition types" (p. 215).

2. Duncan and Rodgers, 1988.

3. Krein and Beller, 1988; Hill and Duncan, 1987; McLanahan, 1985.

4. Bane and Ellwood, 1984; U.S. House of Representatives, Committee on Ways and Means, 1985.

Chapter 2: The Changing Economic Status of Black Children

1. The poverty index is a set of threshold values that differ by family size and composition (number of adults and number of children). Families of a certain size and composition whose family income is below the specified threshold value are officially defined as poor. Because poverty is defined roughly in terms of nutritional needs, poverty threshold values reflect the estimated cost of food for families of different sizes and composition (Miller and Tomaskovic-Devey, 1983). In recent years there has been considerable discussion about changing the definition of poverty (Rexroat and Weber, 1992; Allen and Simms, 1990), although there is no consensus on the proposed changes. Some analysts argue that the dollar value of noncash benefits such as food stamps and Medicaid should be included as income, while others suggest that the increased proportion of family income spent on housing and childcare should be accounted for in the calculation of poverty rates.

2. U.S. Bureau of the Census, 1985b.

3. Vroman, 1989.

4. Long and DeAre, 1982.

5. Lichter, 1988.

6. Rexroat, 1989.

7. Fusfeld and Bates, 1984.

8. Rexroat, 1989. Three other SMSAs contained 100,000 or more blacks in 1980 but were not defined as SMSAs in 1970: Newport News, Nassau-Suffolk County, and Raleigh-Durham (which consisted of two separate SMSAs in 1970, neither of which had a sizable black population).

9. It should be noted that in the Census or CPS data, poverty levels are not adjusted for differences in the cost of living across regions or metro areas.

10. Statistical analysis shows that changes in black employment rates, at the SMSA level, explain more of the variations in child poverty than do changes in children's living arrangements. (See chapter six for a fuller discussion of regional economic conditions and black family income.) While the proportion of black children living in female-headed families did increase in the South during this period, in three-fourths of the Southern metropolitan areas studied this trend was not statistically correlated with changes in black child poverty rates.

11. The 1990 Census data tapes were not available when this study was being conducted; thus certain kinds of information about black children could not be determined. Although the Census Bureau periodically publishes some data on metropolitan areas, one cannot determine the composition of black child poverty and the kind of female-headed family in which black children live without manipulating Census data tapes.

12. CPS data were used to obtain this information for 1984, and the sample sizes are too small to obtain reliable figures at the SMSA level. When the 1990 Census data are available, it will be possible to examine change in the economic status of black children at the metropolitan level from 1980 to 1990.

13. See, for example, Beaulieu, 1988; O'Hare, 1988; Lichter, 1988.

14. Between 1983 and 1985, the Census Bureau redefined the areas it designated as metropolitan and nonmetropolitan, moving about 28 percent of the population formerly designated as nonmetro into the metro category (O'Hare, 1988). The redefinition of these areas was not used in Current Population Survey data until July 1985 (U.S. Bureau of the Census, 1987b). Since data for this study used the March 1985 CPS data, changes in the poverty status of black children shown in tables 2.5 and 2.6 are not affected by the reclassification of nonmetro areas.

15. Durant and Knowlton, 1978.

16. Employment-related hardship is a composite measure consisting of the sum of the unemployed, those no longer looking for work because they believe none is available, the involuntarily part-time employed, and those whose labor market earnings in the past year (adjusted for weeks worked) are less than 1.25 times the individual poverty threshold. This sum is then divided by the total number of workers. Thus workers either are adequately employed or are included in a hardship category that defines the most severe employment hardship they experience (Lichter, 1989). This measure of employment hardship, or the Labor Utilization Framework (LUF) as it is also known, was developed by and appears in Sullivan (1978), Clogg (1979), and Clogg and Sullivan (1983).

Chapter 4 : The Impact of Family Structure on Child Poverty

1. National Center for Health Statistics, 1988.

2. Hofferth, 1985.

3. U.S. Bureau of the Census, 1988.

4. U.S. House of Representatives, Committee on Ways and Means, 1985.

5. U.S. Bureau of the Census, 1986b.

6. Farley and Allen, 1987. As Chapter 6 shows, dramatic increases in the labor force participation of married black mothers since 1960 have contributed to the growing difference in income levels between married-couple and female-headed families.

7. U.S. Bureau of the Census, 1986a; 1973.

8. See Espenshade, 1985, and Farley, 1986. While demographic factors are important for understanding changes in family structure, they generally occur within a broader context of economic, political, and social trends. Recent explanations for changing patterns of marriage and childbearing among blacks include the growth of income transfers (e.g., Aid to Families with Dependent Children) (Murray, 1984), and the rise in black male joblessness (Wilson and Neckerman, 1986). For a review and critique of these explanations, see Wilson (1987) on the welfare hypotheses and McCrate (1988) for black male joblessness.

9. The proportion of all black never-married heads who are under the age of 20 is very small, and has steadily declined since 1960 (from 4.2% in 1960 to 2.1% in 1985).

10. Among whites, by contrast, rising divorce rates are largely responsible for the increase in female-headed families. However, about 12 percent of white female heads with children were never married in 1985 (U.S. Bureau of the Census, 1986a). This level of female headship is much lower than that of blacks, but it does represent an increase in the percentage of this family type among whites. Unlike blacks, however, growth in the proportion of never-married white female heads is largely due to an increase in out-of-

wedlock birth rates (Espenshade, 1983). Between 1970 and 1985, the out-of-wedlock birth rate for whites (the number of births per 1,000 unmarried white women ages 15 to 44) increased from 13.8 to 21.8 (National Center for Health Statistics, 1987).

11. The proportion of children living with relatives as part of a subfamily unit averaged 5 to 6 percent from 1960 to 1980 but rose to 11 percent by 1985. However, about four-fifths of this increase was due to improved Census Bureau procedures in identifying subfamilies, rather than to an actual increase in the proportion of children living in related subfamilies (Bane and Ellwood, 1984a; U.S. Bureau of The Census, 1985a). Therefore, it is difficult to examine trends affecting these children in particular.

12. Although the proportion of black children in dependent-poor families is nearly constant in 1969 and 1979 within family types (table 4.4), the proportion increased slightly at the aggregate level (table 2.2). This is because a growing proportion of black children lived in female-headed families which are more likely to receive public assistance than married-couple families are.

13. One recent study (Beller and Graham, 1986) indicates that only 12 percent of never-married black women with children were awarded child support from the absent father, compared with 49 percent of formerly married black women.

Chapter 5: The Impact of Family Structure on Income

1. However, at the end of the period studied, the median family income of black children in families was about half that of comparable white children ($28,988 and $14,879, respectively, in 1985) (U.S. House of Representatives, Select Committee on Children, Youth, and Families, 1987).

Chapter 6: Factors Affecting Family Income

1. The descriptive data presented in this chapter suggest only the extent of each factor's relative contribution to the deteriorating eco-

nomic status of black children. Sophisticated statistical analyses would more precisely show the relative effects of the four factors. Because of the excessive cost, however, such analyses were not possible.

2. Many analysts (e.g., Murray 1984) argue that growth in transfer incomes is primarily responsible for increased out-of-wedlock childbearing and the growing rate of mother-only families. However, most research finds very little evidence to support these hypotheses/assertions. For a review of these studies, see Wilson and Neckerman (1986).

3. Rank, 1989.

4. Shuptrine and Grant, 1988: 1-2.

5. U.S. House of Representatives, Select Committee on Children, Youth, and Families, 1985.

6. 1959 figures are not shown here, because public assistance income was combined with other unearned income (e.g., Social Security) into one income variable on the 1960 Census data tapes.

7. Edelman, 1987.

8. Counted income includes earnings minus allowances, plus unearned income.

9. U.S. House of Representatives, Committee on Ways and Means, 1985.

10. In approximately three-fourths of all female-headed families with related adults, at least one of these adults was employed.

11. Bowen and Finegan, 1969; Sweet, 1973; Tienda and Glass, 1985.

12. Billingsley, 1973; Stack, 1974.

13. O'Hare, 1988.

14. Congressional Budget Office, 1988.

15. Freeman and Holzer, 1986.

16. Johnson et al., 1988.

17. Wilson, 1987; Congressional Budget Office, 1988; Johnson et al., 1988.

18. Lillard and Magunovich, 1989; Freeman, 1979.

19. Bluestone and Harrison, 1982.

20. Johnson et al., 1988.

21. *Ibid.*

22. *Ibid.*

23. Wilson, 1987.

24. That is, 57.5 percent of all black never-married heads were in their 20s, and 52 percent of these heads in their 20s lived in the Northeast or the Midwest. Thus, .575 x .52 = .299, the proportion of all black never-married female heads who were 20 to 29 years old and who lived in the Northeast or Midwest.

Chapter 7: The Growing Vulnerability of Black Children: Policy Implications

1. Very few black children live in families with a head under the age of 20; only about 0.5 percent did so in 1985.

2. Bane and Ellwood, 1984a; 1984b.

3. This estimate is derived from age-specific poverty rates for black children living with never-married women in 1980. The ratio of the total child-years of poverty to the total child-years was computed

and then multiplied by 17 to obtain the desired estimate of expected number of years of childhood poverty for black children in this family type.

4. DeParle, 1992.

5. McFate, 1991.

6. National Commission on Children, 1991.

7. See the Manpower Demonstration Research Corporation's series of final state reports on the Demonstration of State Work/Welfare Initiatives, covering the states of Arkansas (1985), California (1986), Illinois (1987), Maine (1988), Maryland (1985; 1987 supplement), New Jersey (1988), Virginia (1986), and West Virginia (1986) (Manpower Demonstration Research Corporation, 1985-1988). See also Nightingale et al., 1991.

8. A U.S. Government Accounting Office survey (1991b) of all state JOBS administrators showed, for example, that: (1) over half of the states have experienced or expect to experience shortages in basic/remedial education programs and over 40 percent reported or expected statewide shortages of high school equivalency and job-skills training programs; (2) in more than two-thirds of the states, the supply of childcare and transportation was or was expected to be inadequate to serve JOBS participants; and (3) budget cutbacks in nearly three-fifths of the states have lowered or were expected to lower levels of spending on the JOBS program.

9. U.S. Government Accounting Office, 1991a.

10. *Ibid.*

11. *Ibid.*

12. Moffit, 1990.

13. McLanahan, 1985; Moore et al., 1986.

Works Cited

Allen, Joyce E. and Margaret C. Simms. 1990. "Is a New Yardstick Needed to Measure Poverty?" *Focus* (Joint Center for Political and Economic Studies) 18, No. 2: 6-8.

Bane, Mary Jo. 1986. "Household Composition and Poverty." In Sheldon H. Danziger and Daniel H. Weinberg (eds.), *Fighting Poverty: What Works and What Doesn't.* Cambridge, Mass.: Harvard University Press.

Bane, Mary Jo, and David T. Ellwood. 1984a. "The Dynamics of Children's Living Arrangements." Working paper, Harvard University.

_____. 1984b. "Single Mothers and Their Living Arrangements." Working paper, Harvard University.

Beaulieu, Lionel J., ed. 1988. *The Rural South in Crisis.* Boulder, Colo.: Westview.

Beller, Andrea H. and J.W. Graham. 1986. "The Determinants of Child Support Income." *Social Science Quarterly* 67, No. 2.

Billingsley, Andrew. 1973. "Black Family Structure: Myths and Realities." In *Studies in Public Welfare*, a volume of studies prepared for the Joint Economic Committee of Congress. Washington, D.C.: U.S. Government Printing Office.

Bluestone, Barry and Bennett Harrison. 1982. *The Deindustrialization of America.* New York: Basic Books.

Bowen, William G. and T. Aldrich Finegan. 1969. *The Economics of Labor Force Participation.* Princeton: Princeton University Press.

Brazzell, Jan F., Irving Lefberg and Wolfgang Opitz. 1989. "The Impact of Population Size and the Economy on Welfare Caseloads: The Special Case of Welfare Reform." Paper presented at the annual meeting of the Population Association of America.

Center for Law and Social Policy. 1989. "Family Support Act Mandates Education." *The Partnership* 2 (Winter): 1-4.

Congressional Budget Office. 1988. *Trends in Family Income: 1970-1986.* Washington, D.C.: U.S. Government Printing Office.

Clogg, Clifford C. 1979. *Measuring Underemployment: Demographic Indicators for the United States.* New York: Academic Press.

Clogg, Clifford C. and Teresa A. Sullivan. 1983. "Labor Force Composition and Underemployment Trends, 1969-1980." *Social Indicators Research* 12: 117-52.

DeParle, Jason. 1992. "Why Marginal Changes Don't Rescue the Welfare System." *New York Times*, March 1: E-3.

Duncan, Greg J. and Willard L. Rodgers. 1988. "Longitudinal Aspects of Childhood Poverty." *Journal of Marriage and the Family* 50: 1007-21.

Durant, Thomas J., Jr., and Clark S. Knowlton. 1978. "Rural Ethnic Minorities: Adaptive Response to Inequality." In T.R. Ford (ed.), *Rural U.S.A.: Persistence and Change.* Ames, Iowa: Iowa State University Press.

Edelman, Marian Wright. 1987. *Families in Peril: An Agenda for Social Change.* Cambridge: Harvard University Press.

Espenshade, Thomas J. 1983. "Nuptiality in America: Recent Trends and Future Prospects." Working paper, The Urban Institute.

_____. 1985. "Marriage Trends in America: Estimates, Implications and Underlying Causes." *Population and Development Review* 11: 193-245.

Farley, Reynolds. 1986. "The Black Family: Recent Trends in the Marital Status and Family Status of Blacks and Whites" (Report No. 5). Report to the National Academy of Sciences' Committee on the Status of Black Americans.

Farley, Reynolds and Walter R. Allen. 1987. *The Color Line and the Quality of Life in America.* New York: The Russell Sage Foundation.

Freeman, Richard B. 1979. "The Effect of Demographic Factors on Age-Earnings Profiles." Journal of Human Resources. 14: 289-318.

Freeman, Richard B. and Harry J. Holzer. 1986. *The Black Youth Employment Crisis.* Chicago: The University of Chicago Press.

Fusfeld, Daniel R. and Timothy Bates. 1984. *The Political Economy of the Urban Ghetto.* Carbondale, Ill.: Southern Illinois University Press.

Garfinkel, Irwin and Sara S. McLanahan. 1986. *Single Mothers and Their Children: A New American Dilemma.* Washington, D.C.: The Urban Institute.

Hill, Martha S. and Greg J. Duncan. 1987. "Parental Family Income and the Socioeconomic Attainment of Children." *Social Science Research* 16: 39-73.

Hofferth, Sandra L. 1985. "Updating Children's Life Course." *Journal of Marriage and the Family* 47: 93-116.

Johnson, Clifford M., Andrew M. Sum, and James D. Weill. 1988. *Vanishing Dreams: The Growing Economic Plight of America's Young Families.* Washington, D.C.: Children's Defense Fund; Boston, Mass.: Center for Labor Market Studies, Northeastern University.

Krein, Sheila Fitzgerald and Andrea H. Beller. 1988. "Educational Attainment of Children from Single-Parent Families: Differences by Exposure, Gender, and Race." *Demography* 25: 221-34.

Lichter, Donald T. 1988. "Racial Differences in Underemployment in American Cities." *Americal Journal of Sociology* 93: 771-92.

_____. 1989. "Race, Employment Hardship, and Inequality in the American Nonmetropolitan South." *American Sociological Review* 54: 436-46.

Lillard, Lee A. and Diane J. Magunovich. 1989. "Why the Baby Bust Cohorts Haven't Boomed Yet: A Reconsideration of Cohort Variables in Labor Market Analyses." Presented at the annual meeting of the Population Association of America.

Logan, John R. and Mark Schneider. 1984. "Racial Segregation and Racial Change in American Suburbs." *American Journal of Sociology* 89: 874-88.

Long, Larry H. and Dianne DeAre. 1982. "The Economic Base of Recent Population Growth in Nonmetropolitan Settings." Paper presented at the annual meeting of the Association of American Geographers.

Manpower Demonstration Research Corporation (MDRC). 1985-1988. The Demonstration of State Work/Welfare Initiatives report series. New York: MDRC.

McCrate, Elaine. 1988. "Labor Market Segmentation and Relative Black/White Teenage Birth Rates." Working paper, The Mary Ingraham Bunting Institute, Radcliffe College.

McFate, Katherine. 1991. "Poverty, Inequality, and the Crisis of Social Policy: Summary of Findings." Washington, D.C.: Joint Center for Political and Economic Studies.

McFate, Katherine. 1988. *The Metropolitan Area Factbook: A Statistical Profile of Blacks and Whites in Urban America.* Washington, D.C.: Joint Center for Political Studies.

McLanahan, Sara. 1985. "Family Structure and the Reproduction of Poverty." *American Journal of Sociology* 90: 873-901.

McLaughlin, Diane K. and Carolyn Sachs. 1988. "Poverty in Female-Headed Households: Residential Differences." *Rural Sociology* 53: 287-306.

Miller, S. M., and Donald Tomaskovic-Devey. 1983. *Recapitalizing America: Alternatives to the Corporate Distortion of National Policy.* Boston: Routledge and Kegan Paul.

Moffit, Robert. 1990. "Incentive Effects of the U.S. Welfare System: A Review" (Special Report No. 48). Madison, Wis.: Institute for Research on Poverty.

Moore, Kristin A., Margaret C. Simms, and Charles L. Betsey. 1986. *Choice and Circumstance: Racial Differences in Adolescent Sexuality and Fertility.* New Brunswick, N.J.: Transaction Books.

Murray, Charles. 1984. *Losing Ground: American Social Policy, 1950-1980.* New York: Basic Books.

National Center for Health Statistics. 1972. Monthly Vital Statistics Reports, Vol. 21. Washington, D.C.

_____. 1987a. Monthly Vital Statistics Reports, Vol. 36. Washington, D.C.

_____. 1987b. Vital Statistics of the United States, 1960-1985, Vol. 1, *Natality.* Washington, D.C.

_____. 1988. "Advance Report of Final Natality Statistics, 1986." Monthly Vital Statistics Report, Supplement. Washington, D.C.

National Commission on Children. 1991. "Beyond Rhetoric: A New American Agenda for Children and Families." Washington, D.C.: U.S. Government Printing Office.

Nightingale, Demetra, Douglas Wissoker, Lynn Burbridge, D. Lee Bawden, and Neal Jeffries. 1991. "Evaluation of the Massachusetts Employment and Training Program" (Urban Institute Report 91-1). Washington, D.C.: The Urban Institute Press.

O'Hare, William. 1988. *The Rise of Poverty in Rural America.* Washington, D.C.: Population Reference Bureau.

Rank, Mark R. 1989. "Fertility Among Women on Welfare: Incidence and Determinants." *American Sociological Review* 54: 296- 304.

Rexroat, Cynthia. 1989. "Economic Transformation, Family Structure, and Poverty Rates of Black Children in Metropolitan Areas." *American Economic Review* 79 (American Economic Association Papers and Proceedings): 67-70.

Rexroat, Cynthia and Lynn Weber. 1992. "Racial Inequality and Poverty in Memphis and Five Comparison Cities: Assessing the Costs." Memphis: Center for Research on Women, Memphis State University.

Shaw, Lois B. 1982. "High School Completion for Young Women." *Journal of Family Issues* 3: 147-63.

Shuptrine, Sarah C. and Vicki C. Grant. 1988. "Study of the AFDC/ Medicaid Eligibility Process in the Southern States." Washington, D.C.: Southern Governors' Association.

Simms, Margaret C. 1988. "The Choices that Young Black Women Make: Education, Employment, and Family Formation." Paper presented at the Wellesley College Conference on the Economic Condition of Black Women, March 24-25.

Stack, Carol B. 1974. *All Our Kin: Strategies for Survival in a Black Community.* New York: Harper and Row.

Sullivan, Teresa A. 1978. *Marginal Workers, Marginal Jobs.* Austin, Texas: University of Texas Press.

Sweet, James A. 1973. *Women in the Labor Force.* New York: Academic Press.

Tienda, Marta and Jennifer Glass. 1985. "Household Structure and Labor Force Participation of Black, Hispanic, and White Mothers." *Demography* 22: 381-94.

U.S. Bureau of the Census. 1970. "Household and Family Characteristics". Current Population Reports, Series P-20, No. 212. Washington, D.C.: U.S. Government Printing Office.

_____. 1973. "U.S. Summary, Detailed Characteristics." *Census of the Population and Housing,* Vol. 1, Part 1. Washington, D.C.: U.S. Government Printing Office.

_____. 1985a. "Marital Status and Living Arrangements: March 1984." Current Population Reports, Series P-20, No. 399. Washington, D.C.: U.S. Government Printing Office.

_____. 1985b. "Money Income and Poverty Status of Families and Persons in the United States: 1987." Current Population Reports. Series P-60, No. 161. Washington, D.C.: U.S. Government Printing Office.

_____. 1985c. "Household and Family Characteristics." Current Population Reports, Series P-20, No. 411. Washington, D.C.: U.S. Government Printing Office.

_____. 1986a. "Household and Family Characteristics: March 1985." Current Population Reports, Series P-20, No. 410. Washington, D.C.: U.S. Government Printing Office.

_____. 1986b. "Marital Status and Living Arrangements: March 1985." Current Population Reports, Series P-20, No. 411. Washington, D.C.: U.S. Government Printing Office.

_____. 1987a. "Money Income of Households, Families, and Persons in the United States: 1986." Current Population Reports, Series P-60, No. 159. Washington, D.C.: U.S. Government Printing Office.

_____. 1987b. "Poverty in the United States: 1985." Current Population Reports, Series P-60, No. 158. Washington, D.C.: U.S. Government Printing Office.

_____. 1988. "Money Income and Poverty Status of Families and Persons in the United States: 1987." Current Population Reports, Series P-60, No. 161. Washington, D.C.: U.S. Government Printing Office.

U.S. Government Accounting Office. 1991a. "Mother-Only Families: Low Earnings Will Keep Many Children in Poverty." HRD-91-62 (April). Washington, D.C.

_____. 1991b. "Welfare to Work: States Begin JOBS But Fiscal and Other Problems May Impede Their Progress." HRD-91-106 (September). Washington, D.C.

U.S. House of Representatives, Committee on Ways and Means. 1985. "Children in Poverty." Washington, D.C.: U.S. Government Printing Office.

U.S. House of Representatives, Select Committee on Children, Youth, and Families. 1987. "U.S. Children and Their Families: Current Conditions and Recent Trends." Washington, D.C.: U.S. Government Printing Office.

Vroman, Wayne. 1989. "Industrial Change and Black Men's Relative Earnings." Working paper, The Urban Institute.

Wilson, William J. 1987. *The Truly Disadvantaged.* Chicago: University of Chicago Press.

Wilson, William J. and Kathryn M. Neckerman. 1986. "Poverty and Family Structure: The Widening Gap between Evidence and Public Policy Issues." In Sheldon H. Danziger and Daniel H. Weinberg (eds.), *Fighting Poverty: What Works and What Doesn't.* Cambridge, Mass.: Harvard University Press.

About the Author

Cynthia Rexroat is an associate professor of sociology and research professor at the Center for Research on Women, Memphis State University. She was a research associate at the Joint Center for Political and Economic Studies when she carried out the study for this book. Her current work includes examinations of the employment of women heads of household and of racial differences in attitudes toward welfare.

Joint Center Board of Governors